Education in the
Twenty-first Century

T0124845

*The Hoover Institution gratefully acknowledges
the following individuals and foundations for their
significant support of the*

Initiative
on
American Public Education

KORET FOUNDATION
TAD AND DIANNE TAUBE
LYNDE AND HARRY BRADLEY FOUNDATION
BOYD AND JILL SMITH
JACK AND MARY LOIS WHEATLEY
FRANKLIN AND CATHERINE JOHNSON
JERRY AND PATTI HUME
DORIS AND DONALD FISHER
BERNARD LEE SCHWARTZ FOUNDATION

*The Hoover Institution
gratefully acknowledges*

SHERM AND MARGE TELLEEN

*for their generous support
of this book project.*

Education in the Twenty-first Century

EDITOR
Edward P. Lazear

CONTRIBUTING AUTHORS
Robert J. Barro
Gary S. Becker
Andrew J. Coulson
Robert E. Hall
Edward P. Lazear
Jennifer Roback Morse
Paul M. Romer
George P. Shultz
Thomas Sowell
Shelby Steele

HOOVER INSTITUTION PRESS
STANFORD UNIVERSITY   STANFORD, CALIFORNIA

www.hoover.org

Hoover Institution Press Publication No. 501

First printing 2002

07 06 05 04 03 02   9 8 7 6 5 4 3 2 1

Manufactured in the United States of America

The paper used in this publication meets the minimum requirements
of the American National Standard for Information Sciences—
Permanence of Paper for Printed Library Materials, ANSI
Z39.48–1984.

Library of Congress Cataloging-in-Publication Data

Education in the twenty-first century / editor, Edward P. Lazear ;
contributing authors, Robert J. Barro ... [et al.].
      p. cm.
Includes bibliographical references (p.) and index.
   ISBN 0-8179-2892-8 (alk. paper)
   1. Education and state--United States. 2. Educational planning--
United States. 3. Education--Economic aspects--United States.
4. Education--Social aspects--United States. I. Title: Education in
the 21st century. II. Lazear, Edward P. III. Barro, Robert J.
   LC89 .E26 2002
   379.73--dc21
                                        2002000808

Contents

Director's Foreword

John Raisian

The Hoover Institution is currently engaged in nine focused public policy research initiatives, the most ambitious of which is titled *American Public Education*. As Americans, we are increasingly concerned about the academic performance of our children and the structure and organization of our elementary and secondary school systems. The purpose of this Hoover initiative is to examine issues on education policy, offering *ideas defining a free society*—in this instance, recommendations on education policy designed to bring about positive improvement in K–12 education consistent with the founding principles of our free society.

We at Hoover are grateful to Hoover fellow Edward Lazear for organizing this volume and to the team of scholars who contributed their thoughts; they are an august group to weigh in on this subject. This effort serves not only as part of a number of offerings on education policy but also as the first of a projected series that will address major themes associated with long-term trends and public policy formation. Such a series is conceived as collecting thoughts on the big picture associated with trends and concerns that will impact Americans. We must begin a dialogue sooner rather than later, but the dissemination of ideas about long-term trends and the formation of long-term policy are perhaps the most difficult tasks we face as a society. Whereas much attention is brought to bear on the short-term crisis, we seek to alter the balance by introducing a "big idea" series.

The investment of society's resources in quality human-capital accumulation is the subject of this volume. We hope that the contributors to this volume will set the course for effective ideas that will positively impact the value of our human resources and, in so doing, raise the quality of life for all citizens.

Foreword

George P. Shultz

The Hoover Institution was founded to study war, revolution, and peace. Quite obviously, such an agenda must lead to education: education for the citizen, education to understand the causes of war and the imperatives of peace, to know the nature of revolutions, and to be able to cope and earn a living in whatever world you inhabit.

Such an orientation also recognizes that access to education must be available to every child, whatever the background of the parents may be. And beyond universality, you look for quality. The least common denominator in education is not at all satisfactory. Every child must be able to achieve his or her utmost potential. So quality must be an integral part of broadly available opportunity. Simple and sensible, yes, but it would be revolutionary if these objectives were realized.

Over the past few decades, however, we have seen increasing recognition of the importance of education and of the huge range of quality that exists in our system: compare precollegiate with higher education; compare the quality of education offered in different parts of our country; and compare it in areas of varying levels of income per capita. Too many precollegiate schools, probably one-half to two-thirds, are failing to educate students up to any reasonable standard of adequacy.

What can we do to remedy this situation? And remedy it we must, not simply in the interests of the children themselves but to ensure the healthy operation of our society. We live in a new age, variously characterized, but probably aptly described as the knowledge age. In such an age, studies by economists over several decades that show the high rate of return to education would be likely to show even higher returns. To put the point in reverse fashion, they would be likely to show that those without an education or with a low-quality education are unable to take advantage of opportunities and to cope adequately with the new environment of the knowledge age.

That new environment creates all sorts of challenges to the process of education itself. Children learn all day long and not only in the classroom. They have access through their nimble fingers to computer and television screens that contain an astonishing and escalating array of ideas and information. At the same time, within the school environment and what is traditionally called "homework," there is tremendous room to use new means to stimulate and broaden the process of learning.

Recent years, then, have seen this culmination of forces: the recognition of the failures in our schools, the transcendent importance of correcting those problems, and the new opportunities for learning presented by the new technologies.

So scholars at the Hoover Institution have turned to this subject in a concentrated way. The present effort builds on a tremendous background. Three decades ago, in their classic *Capitalism and Freedom*, Milton and Rose Friedman foresaw the problem and wrote compellingly about the desirability of giving all parents, not just wealthy ones, a choice of where their children go to school and about the virtues of introducing the idea of a competitive marketplace to the process of education. These days, this idea of choice—in a halting manner, to be sure—seems to be taking hold. Certainly attention is being focused on what should be done.

Suppose you have the task of designing a system of precollegiate education for the United States and you can start with a clean slate. What would you propose? Where would you start? You know the new technologies can make a difference in what your child needs from the school and what can be obtained elsewhere. You know that there is a wide scope for use of these technologies in the schools themselves. However much you are impressed with the new technology, you would certainly begin with a few of the things that we all know from our experiences and common observation:

1. Parents, by and large, care about their children and have a shrewd sense of what is good for them. So base the system on parental control. Advice from professionals can help, but such experts often disagree. When they agree, they tend to be trendy, and trends change. Who is to choose among the various offerings? Let the parents do the choosing! Of course, some may argue that not all parents care and that some children have effectively been abandoned by their parents. Even in those tragic cases, however, the effort by most parents to choose can have a positive impact on the quality of the schools and thereby benefit all children in the schools.

2. Parents know that certain basic skills are essential to reasonable life prospects. Comfortable use of the English language, written and spoken, is primary.

A second language is certainly desirable, especially Spanish, since it is so widely used in our country. But the key is English, starting as early in life as possible. Certainly English should be the language spoken in the schools.

In California recently, an initiative to ban bilingual education in the state's public schools passed overwhelmingly, receiving 61 percent of the vote. This initiative was opposed by the teachers unions and the educational establishment, but results are already pouring in. Children learn rapidly, and their ability to master English comes quickly and is tremendously beneficial to them. Here, parents who expressed themselves at the voting booth turned out to have a greater sense of what's good for their children than did the educational establishment.

3. As essential as English is the language of numbers and the ability to use numbers. Beyond sheer arithmetic are the abstractions of mathematics, essential in themselves but also a prime way to develop a child's power to reason.

So the language of reading and writing and the language of figuring and reasoning are the essential underpinnings for students to gain access to the vast array of substance that we call "education." There's nothing new, nothing revolutionary, in this idea, enshrined as it is in the mythology of "readin', writin', and 'rithmetic." Beyond these skills and their use, education, a continuous process, includes values and priorities. In this regard, reflection on many of my own learning processes leads me to sports, military service, business, church, my family, and to the opportunity for public service. I won't go through all these areas; let me use just one example taken from sports.

A great value that everyone must learn is the importance of accountability. Many people spend their lives trying to avoid accountability, but life is much more satisfying if you learn how to step up to it. In golf, the process is relentless. There you are on the putting green with a putter in your hand. After receiving whatever advice you're entitled to, you are the one who has to decide on the speed and the break. You are the one who hits the ball. When the ball stops rolling, the result is unambiguous; the ball is in the cup or it is not in the cup. Relentless accountability—a great lesson for life.

To return to our clean slate, we start with a lot of evidence. We know that competition works in field after field. The effects of competition are to lower costs, to increase quality, and to provide consumers with choices as diverse as their varied tastes. There is no reason why this principle should not apply to the process of education.

One piece of evidence readily available to us is the great experiment in competition and choice that took place in our country immediately following World War II. Here came the vets, I among them, who had the benefits of the G.I. Bill. We could go anywhere and have tuition paid while receiving a small stipend to help with living expenses. We and our parents were the choosers. A multitude of serious young people entered the system of higher education with high aspirations and sudden velocity. They were in college to learn, not to play around. This competitive environment hit a system of higher education that had spent four or five years somewhat on the shelf as young people went to war or to work. The result was electric and long-lasting; it was, in fact, a revolution. Today, we have the world's best system of higher education, a system characterized by great diversity. Publicly supported schools still predominate in terms of numbers of students attending, and the schools' quality level has been raised by the competitive process. Why shouldn't this process work just as well in the K–12 arena?

We see the problem when we move from our clean slate to the real world. We encounter huge institutional rigidities that are firmly in place and that possess formidable political capability. Change, we know, is always difficult, but persistence is essential to a revolution that will eventually follow the weight of evidence. And evidence is piling up that choice and competition produce superior results for students in their precollegiate years. That is why parents who can afford to do so often move to areas where there are good public schools. That is why parochial schools flourish

in low-income-per-capita areas and produce demonstrably
superior results. That is why a wide variety of private
schools have emerged to compete with one another as well
as with the public school system. That is why people who
live in low-income-per-capita areas are increasingly drawn to
the possibilities of enhancing their children's opportunities
through exercising a choice.

Consider these facts: One in four children enrolled in a
private K–12 school in this country—one in four—comes
from a household with an income of less than $35,000 per
year. Another 20 percent come from households with incomes of less than $50,000 per year. More than half the
children in parochial schools come from households with
an income of less than $35,000 per year and one in ten
from households with less than $15,000 per year. The par-
ents of all these children have to put up some money to
send their children to these schools. Certainly there are
scholarships, but parents still need to pay a portion of the
tuition—and they pay in after-tax dollars.

In the Children's Scholarship Fund, an effort initiated by
two creative philanthropists, Teddy Forstmann and John
Walton, private scholarships go, in effect, only to children
from low-income households. The applicant has to put up
$1,000 to supplement this private scholarship. The Fund
has been absolutely inundated with over 1.25 million applications—and from households with low incomes that
are going to have to put up $1,000!

You have to ask yourself what the reason is for this. The
answer is clear. Caring and observant parents can easily
see what is taking place. People who have the resources to
do so live in areas where there are good schools, good in
part because there is heavy parental involvement in them.
These parents have the financial capacity to exercise a
choice, and they do so. If they don't like the public school,
they have the capacity to pay double, that is, to pay their
taxes for a public school and then pay again to send their
children to a private school, and many do just that.

People in low-income-per-capita areas have observed this and are becoming more knowledgeable about it. A revolution in their thinking is underway. They are beginning to realize, more and more, that a system of choice is not about children of wealthy parents; it's about them, because the wealthy children already have a choice. They want to be able to exercise a choice, too. They think that they, as parents, can make a better choice than the people operating the public education monopoly.

Let me take you finally to a different subject: Social Security. Our Social Security system was designed under the guidance of Franklin Roosevelt, a shrewd politician. A lot of thought went into the way the system was set up. Roosevelt saw clearly that, to work over a long period of time, Social Security could not be looked upon in any way as a welfare system. To work, Social Security payments had to be a matter of right. He encouraged the notion that, if you pay into something, you will get something out. With all due respect to the mythology of the Social Security system, the reality is that you do have money deducted from your paycheck. The money goes into something called "Social Security," and you do have benefits that are calculated somewhat in relation to your level of payments. The payments are a matter of right. It's not a matter of whether you're poor or not; it's a matter of right.

I think that education needs to be considered in the same way, that having an educational opportunity that is in considerable part publicly funded, in this case from taxes levied at the state and community levels, is a matter of right. But it should also be a matter of right that you, the taxpayer and the citizen, have control over where you spend that money because you, the parent, care about your child and you want to guide that child to the place of learning that will be most beneficial.

Experimentation and experience are rapidly producing increasing evidence of what works and what does not work. Hoover scholars will continue the search for the right answers, looking at evidence, accumulating insights, and presenting a wide variety of ideas, as they do in this volume. In the end, what matters most to young people and to our society is this simple maxim: the child comes first; use what works and throw out what fails the child. This simple maxim presents a compelling measure of the need for change, for to follow it would amount to a revolution!

Introduction

Edward P. Lazear

This book is an outgrowth of the desire at the Hoover Institution to focus on issues that are of essential policy relevance. Right now, few issues are more important in the
United States than improving education. This introduction
summarizes the key arguments made in the book's essays.
The summary is followed by a discussion of some of the
key policy questions in education. More will be said on the
nature of the book below, but let us get to the essence first.

THE IMPORTANCE OF EDUCATION

In his Foreword, George P. Shultz states that education is
failing too many of our students. It is essential to remedy
the situation, he goes on to say, because there is simply too
much at stake. On the whole, parents know what is good
for their own children. The usual argument for limiting
parental discretion is that there are certain parents who
neglect their children or who simply do not have the information necessary to make the appropriate decisions. Although this is true, Shultz points out that even were this the
case, as long as a significant fraction of the population
cares about the quality of their children's education, the

schools will be forced to rise to the standard demanded by diligent parents.

Shultz argues that there are a few themes that should be part of any educational agenda. First, he views English-based education as essential, because English is by far the dominant language in the United States. Children who are not firmly grounded in English will have difficulties throughout their entire lifetimes. Second, accountability is key, and what Shultz means by accountability is not only accountability for the school but accountability for the individual. Students should be held accountable for their actions and for their own education. Third, competition among schools is important because it lowers costs, increases quality, and gives individuals choices. Shultz sees choice as a matter of right. Education in this country should be a right, and the choice about how that education is delivered should be a parental right. In sum, he concludes that the child comes first. We should keep what works and throw out what fails. Indeed, he argues that doing this would be revolutionary.

A natural starting point is to ask, "Why is education so important?" Gary S. Becker points out that human capital is the most important part of the economy, and human capital in large part is produced by formal education. Furthermore, the importance of education has grown in recent decades, and new technology for delivering it, such as distance learning, will help it grow even further.

Becker contrasts human capital with physical capital. Physical capital, that is, the machines, buildings, infrastructures, and tangible assets, while important to the economy, is an overrated factor of production. Becker argues that an appropriate accounting of the capital in society would show that human capital accounts for a much greater portion of the total capital stock than does physical capital. Good evidence for this, he argues, is provided by the crash of the stock market in 1987. The effect on the economy was minimal because it affected primarily physical capital and not human capital. Indeed, because the stock of human capital did not fall during that period, there was not a large drop in the total stock of capital, even if one believes that the market decline reflected a real fall in the value of physical capital.

Although formal education is important, individuals continue to acquire human capital throughout their lifetimes by learning on the job and in other ways. Becker believes that significant growth in the economy will come from increases in human capital, which in turn stimulate technological change.

EDUCATION AND GROWTH

Education can affect technological change through a number of different channels. First, a more educated population may create new technology by inventing more and better things. Second, a more educated population might simply produce more output per unit of time. If education increases over time, then productivity might increase over time, resulting in growth.

A number of authors have examined the relation between growth and education. Two of the most important contributors to the literature have essays included in this book. One, Robert Barro, summarizes comprehensive work that examines many countries over a period of more than three decades. Barro points out that there is an important distinction between the quantity of education and its quality, and that the distinction matters for interpreting and measuring the effects of education on growth. He finds that both quantity and quality affect growth. What do we mean by the quality of education? Barro measures the quality of education by outcome variables, most notably test scores on standardized exams. He argues that test scores are a reflection of educational quality and have effects on economic activity. In particular, science and math test scores have a positive influence on economic growth. Part of these test scores reflects inputs of the school, and part may also reflect culture and the effort of the individual students involved. Hours of work vary significantly by country. Hours of school attendance and homework vary by country as well. No one would be surprised to find that the more input there is, the more output.

Barro argues that human capital is extremely important, primarily in terms of the ability of societies to grasp new technology and to help its diffusion throughout the economy. The larger its stock of human capital, the more quickly a country can use any given amount of new technology. He also argues that physical capital can be changed very rapidly, but that the stock of human capital, which is imbedded in the population, changes only slowly. It is therefore important to make investments in human capital over a significant period of time.

Robert Hall also has examined the effects of education on national output. He does so primarily by focusing on productivity. Hall and Charles Jones have found in other studies that although education does not explain all of the variation in productivity around the world, it is an important determinant of productivity variation. The United States is not the highest in its index of education, but the combination of high levels of education, high investment in physical capital, and high efficiency all contribute to make the United States the most productive country in the world.

Hall believes that much of this is a result of rule of law and infrastructure. When a country's infrastructure is favorable, crime rates are low and the best people produce rather than devote their energies to corruption. One form of investment is investment in human capital, so Hall argues that the correlation that is observed between rule of law and education reflects, at least in part, causation running from the former to the latter.

Given that education has effects on the macroeconomy, it is not surprising that education affects the individuals in the economy. Education's effect on individual income is well known and has been documented in the economics literature consistently for over forty years. Specifically, those who are more educated receive higher earnings, presumably as a result of their increased productivity. Also as a result of higher productivity, educated workers are not as likely to be laid off during cyclical downturns. As a society improves the level of education of the individuals who make it up, that society also creates a wealthier and less vulnerable population. These patterns have been documented over time for virtually every group and country throughout the world. Even individuals in the most disadvantaged groups in a society benefit from higher levels of education. Recent figures from the Current Population Survey (1999) show that the average college graduate in the United States earns about 70 percent more than the average high school graduate.

The structure of schools.   Much of the discussion in the policy arena today revolves around the choice between public and private school structures. The voucher movement is one attempt to use public money to fund private schools in order to obtain the best of both worlds. As Shultz points out in his introduction, most individuals regard education as a right. He also argues, though, that the right to education does not necessarily require that education be provided by public schools, even if they are funded by a public entity such as the locality, state, or federal government. The charter school movement is a partial reaction to the pressure for private schools and vouchers in general.

Andrew Coulson provides an interesting account of private and public education in a historical context. Coulson argues that, surprisingly, the move toward private education is not a modern phenomenon, and furthermore, the historical record provides evidence that private schools actually work better than public schools. He criticizes current educators for having ignored the historical record and cites a number of examples.

In the 1960s and 1970s, the federal government undertook a multibillion-dollar experiment called "Follow Through." The evidence from this study was that direct instruction produced the best outcomes, but the nation ignored the findings.

Coulson believes that the rejection of empirical testing of new methods has contributed to a dismal record of stagnation and decline in achievement over the past one hundred years.

The historical record is quite interesting on this point. In both the United States and in England in the late 1700s and 1800s, a significant majority of citizens could read and write despite the fact that the state played little role in fostering the spread of literacy.

Coulson suggests that schools perform two functions. The first is to further individual goals that make the person a better worker and more able wage earner, creating skills, and simply providing academic knowledge. But in addition, there are social aspects to education that have to do with harmony, participation in the democratic process, and creating equality of educational opportunity. Coulson believes that state schools are actually worse at providing for the social objectives than are private schools, primarily because independent schools serve a diverse community's needs, whereas public schools induce people to fight over the nature of a uniform curriculum. As an example of this, he suggests that state funding, which was introduced into the Muslim world in the eleventh century, eliminated the tolerance that had been enjoyed in Muslim education up to that point. Furthermore, the evidence on comparison between private schools and public schools suggests that public schools tend to be more segregated than private schools. For example, students in private schools are more likely to choose lunch partners from other races than are students in public schools.

As a solution to the problems, Coulson suggests five policy prescriptions: parental choice, parental financial responsibility, freedom for educators, competition between schools, and a profit motive for schools. Unlike many advocates of private schools, Coulson opposes vouchers because he believes they are inconsistent with furthering these five goals. If nothing else, they remove or reduce parental responsibility in providing for the education of their own children. Instead, he proposes privately financed scholarships and philanthropic tax credit programs, which he believes will induce enough giving to fund a significant private sector.

When it comes to educating minorities, Thomas Sowell also criticizes educators for not having looked at the evidence. Sowell states that there is a great deal of evidence that minority students can, and in fact do, perform very well. He provides the example of a number of high schools that performed well despite the fact that the children were poor. Dunbar, in Washington, D.C., Public School 91 in Brooklyn, and St. Augustine, a Catholic school in New Orleans, all fit into this category. These schools have work and discipline in common. Although this is not the only model for success, Sowell believes that there is no reason to assume that because students come from low-income or minority households they will necessarily fail.

Sowell describes his own experience in a school in Harlem. When he was a student, the Harlem schools performed no worse than schools from the lower East Side. In fact, the Harlem schools produced a number of individuals who, like Sowell himself, were very successful. He points out that the black middle class came only from these schools, since initially there was no black middle class. All of the black students went to schools with other poor students.

That having been said, Sowell is concerned that children growing up in Harlem today will not have as great a chance to rise as people of Sowell's generation, primarily because they will not receive the solid education that he received. The problem is exacerbated because education is even more important today than it was when Sowell attended school.

School Funding

Paul Romer asks why vouchers have not been politically successful, even though most economists believe they are an efficient way to fund schooling. Romer's answer is that the delivery system for the product and public support for its financing are not independent. The basic idea is that when parents are confronted with students in their own district who do not do well, they are more likely to vote for public support of education than when they do not encounter those students. A voucher system, he argues, although perhaps efficient, would likely result in less overall funding, and especially less funding of those students who have the greatest need on their own.

Romer argues that there is underinvestment in education because of free-rider effects in any voluntary system of transfers to education. Suppose that a community would like to have a more equal distribution of income and that providing education for economically disadvantaged students is the best way to bring that about. Each person in society may want this to happen, but no one individual has the right incentives to pay for it. Each would prefer to let others pay for education, resulting in overall underfunding of education. To solve the free-rider problem, it is necessary to fund publicly.

The situation is exacerbated by the opening up of trade, which tends to result in even greater pressure for income inequality. As technology moves across borders, those with the highest levels of human capital are most able to take advantage of the new technologies.

Finally, when individuals are separated from those who are in need, their compassion is less likely to result in actual transfers. Thus, programs that tie the welfare of the most disadvantaged to the welfare of those with whom interaction is greatest, namely, our own children, are most likely to generate support.

FAMILY AND EXPECTATIONS

Most recognize that in addition to the school, the family is important in a child's educational development. Jennifer Roback Morse, however, argues that the current structure may actually undermine the ability of the family to augment what is done in schools to develop a child's investment in human capital. The current view, she claims, is that the primary connection between the parents and children is one of a transfer of resources from the parent to the child. Under this view, the school's role is to supplement that transfer by moving resources from schools to children. She argues an alternative view: that the school should enhance, or at the least not undermine, the parent-child relationship.

She points to a number of policies that weaken the relationship between parents and their children. The move toward universal preschool, the push for school breakfast programs, and the hostility of public school systems to home schooling are all policies that make it more difficult for parents to interact with their children. The school becomes a supplier of resources, often in opposition to the interests or wishes of the family.

Morse's essay documents the importance of parental guidance in the development of children. She bases her argument, at least theoretically, on Friedrich Hayek's notion that local control is better than central control because those in the local situation have better information. Using evidence from eastern Europe, Morse documents the difficulties that arise when children are not brought up in a loving family environment. There is significant evidence from the United States that children of single parents are more likely to have problems. If nothing else, the time input alone has an effect, and single parents cannot devote as much time to their children as two parents can, despite the fact that some single parents spend more time with their children than some parent couples.

The point of Morse's discussion is that children need relationships more than they need resources, and the terms of the debate should be shifted. It is silly, she claims, to argue that there is not a hierarchy of family types in terms of effect on the child's subsequent development. The posture of neutrality among family types should be dropped. She believes that the term "broken home," rather than more politically correct expressions, is appropriate. It reflects the poignant reality from the child's perspective that life has been disrupted. In addition to everything else, Morse argues that high parental expectations of children are just as important as the other elements that parents can provide.

So, what are the policies? First, school choice should be encouraged because it forces parents to think about their children's education. Second, policies that crowd out the family should be avoided. For example, we should shift the emphasis away from providing day care toward making it possible to keep mothers at home with their children. Similarly, universal school breakfast programs have detrimental side effects because they allow families to ignore the dysfunction of not having breakfast together. Finally, some policies can actually encourage family involvement with their children. Morse describes a school lunch program where mothers were required to help. If nothing else, this brought the parent to the school once or twice a month. Indeed, other school participatory programs are useful in this context. To the extent possible, parents should be encouraged to be mentors for their children.

A number of authors in this volume mention expectations, and no one focuses on expectations more vividly than does Shelby Steele in his essay entitled "Educating Black Students." Steele tells the story of the fictional Charlie Parker, who cannot learn to play the saxophone because he is from a disadvantaged household without the benefit of a white person's education. The real Charlie Parker, of course, became a premier musical figure without help from whites for two reasons that Steele views as advantages. First, Parker enjoyed the disinterest of the larger society as a whole. Second, he was held to standards of excellence. Steele believes that it is a mistake to make the education of blacks the concern of others. To do so suggests that blacks are inert people. Under such a view, others act, and blacks are acted upon.

Steele defines "agency" as a situation where responsibility is taken over others, as parents do for their children. Thus, parents exercise agency when they select the schools that their children will attend. But agency involves determination and commitment. The first sign that a group has taken agency over an area is that it impersonally enforces a rigorous standard of excellence. Steele argues that black student performance has been weak, not because whites have failed, but because blacks have not taken agency over the academic development of their children as they have in areas such as music and sports. Excellence is demanded in music and sports, standards are high, and blacks succeed. In education, the reverse has been true. Sometimes the culture in the black community actually discourages excellence in academics by calling excellent students "white wannabes." Steele continues to say that the same is true of white America, which has not demanded the same standards of excellence for blacks as it requires of whites. In order to bring about excellent education for minorities, Steele believes that it is essential to enforce personal accountability and the highest standards.

POLICY ISSUES

Is More Money the Solution?

The usual way to deal with problems in the public sector is to assume that increasing expenditures will solve the problem. This has been true in education as much as in any other area. In education, at least in recent years, the focus has been primarily on reduction of class size. But there is a large literature suggesting that altering class size has no effect on outcomes.[1] There are a few studies, however, that do find important class size effects. Alan Krueger (1998, 1999) and Joshua Angrist and Victor Lavy (1999) find that reducing class size has beneficial outcomes. Since reducing class size is one of the key policy proposals at both federal and state levels and since this policy implies very large costs to taxpayers, it is important to understand the data before a blanket policy of class size reduction is introduced.

Why do some studies find effects whereas others do not? The answer to the puzzle is that classroom education is what economists call a "public good." That is, one child can benefit from a teacher's instruction at the same time that another benefits from the same instruction. If both listen attentively to the lesson, then both can obtain the human capital being provided by the teacher.

The problem in the real classroom is that students do not always listen attentively to the teacher's instructions, and in a public-good setting of this sort, when one child acts out, he reduces or eliminates the instructional component of that moment in the classroom for all the other children in the class. Of course, educators are well aware of this, and it is the reason why preschool children are placed in smaller classes than are most college freshmen. (In fact, as an undergraduate at UCLA, I was in a class with two thousand other students who watched the professor on television in four rooms that seated five hundred each.) Much of the controversy can be eliminated once it is understood that education is a public good subject to negative spillovers from each of the students.[2] The difficulty arises from the pairing of better students with larger class sizes. As a result, even if class size effects were important, they would be difficult to observe in data from the real world, because the better-behaved and presumably more able students are in large classes. The less-well-behaved, and presumably younger students, are in smaller classes. When researchers examine large classes, they find that educational outcomes are sometimes better in the large classes than in small classes. The reason, however, is that students are not randomly assigned to these classes but are sorted according to their ability, with the better students in the large classes. So, the failure to observe class size effects may simply be a result of ignoring the fact that larger classes are associated with better students.

To see this, consider an extreme case. Advanced placement students are often found in very large classes because these students are relatively well-behaved and sit quietly through instruction. At the other end of the spectrum are students with behavior disorders, who tend to be placed in small classes. A naive analysis would find the large classes with the able students outperforming the smaller classes with the less able students. This does not mean that reducing class size for the able students would not have beneficial effects, nor does it imply that increasing class size for the disruptive students would not have harmful effects. But it does mean that such effects will not be observed in studies that cut across class sizes.

Does this mean that reducing class size is the solution? Not at all. In fact, the best studies tend to find that to the extent class size effects are important, they are not universal. Disadvantaged children, either as a result of economic status or learning ability, are most likely to benefit from smaller class sizes. Similarly, younger children are also likely to benefit from smaller class size.

Finally, a point made by Eric Hanushek is that teacher quality is an extremely important determinant of educational performance. In fact, in his Texas study, Hanushek finds that putting a child in a good teacher's classroom is much more important in terms of affecting student learning than almost any other factor.

The immediate policy question, then, is how we can raise teacher quality. Although money is not everything, money is almost certain to make a difference in this case. Data from 1999 show that teachers on average earn about 77 percent the salary of the average college graduate. This has resulted in a smaller selection of candidates for teaching jobs than would be the case if teaching salaries were higher. Indeed, Caroline Hoxby at Harvard has shown that the average SAT scores for public school teachers are well below the median for the country as a whole. When the individuals who became teachers were actually applying to college, they themselves were in the lower half of performers on the standard college entrance tests. This is not particularly surprising, since teachers are so poorly paid relative to other college graduates. It is true, of course, that teachers have more leisure during the summer than do individuals in other occupations, but it is also likely that increasing teachers'

salaries would draw a larger number of people to the profession, and schools could then choose more selectively. In
addition, schools would have an easier time replacing those
teachers who turned out to be less-than-effective in the
classroom.

Federal versus Local Administration of Schools

The reality is that most of the money going to education
comes from the state and not from the federal government.
Indeed, the largest federal program accounts for only about
fourteen billion dollars nationwide. The state education
budget in California alone is triple that figure. Thus, it is difficult to expect the federal government to do much to influence education policy, which is made primarily at the state
and local level. There have, however, been some attempts to
use federal muscle to influence local educational decisions.
Before analyzing such policies, it is important to ask whether
having federal policies is appropriate, or whether they are
better left to the state.

There are three arguments against allowing the federal government to play an important role in educational policy. First,
when the federal government is guiding the nation's education
policy, the stakes are much higher than is the case when localities are guiding the education policy. The impact of educational policy at the national level is far greater than that at the
local level. For example, if all schools were required to use the
same textbooks for a particular subject in a particular grade,
the profits associated with inducing a federal level administrator to choose a particular publisher's book would be far
greater than those associated with inducing any single local
administrator to do the same. As a result, lobbying pressure
would be far greater if power was centralized and federal
agencies more subject than local ones to capture.

Second, even if federal authorities make what everyone believes to be the right decision, centralizing decisions to the
federal level creates an extremely risky situation. When deci-

sions are made at the local level, a wrong decision does not result in a nationwide disaster. When decisions are made at the federal level, making a mistake in education policy does not just affect the students in a given locality but could be devastating to an entire generation of the nation's students. Furthermore, there would be no way for Americans to escape such a policy. If a locality made a bad decision, parents who were seeking to improve the welfare of their children at least would have the option of moving out of that locality to another public school setting. Federal requirements would allow no such movement, and competition among districts would be stifled.

Third, unless the federal budget for education is increased dramatically, it is unlikely that policies at the federal level will have the teeth required to get policies implemented. States and localities will be willing to comply with federal policies only insofar as the amount that will be lost by failing to comply exceeds the costs imposed on the districts by the policies themselves. Thus, localities will be willing to make small changes, but the federal government's ability to influence local policy will be greatly limited by small amounts being transferred to localities.

EVALUATION OF SOME SUGGESTED POLICIES

Politicians offer ideas for educational policy changes almost as frequently as they make speeches. A number of those policies are considered here.

National Exams

One of the most frequently mentioned policies is instituting a required national examination. There are a number of positive aspects to this proposal, the most obvious of which is that it would become easier to hold schools accountable for their teaching. If the standard is the same for everyone, then comparison becomes much more straightforward.

The major problem is that a national exam requires centralization. The choice of questions would be hotly debated, because some questions would favor certain groups and teaching philosophies, while others would favor other groups and different teaching philosophies.

Even if a good and just exam were created, the policy would still suffer from the problem of putting all eggs in one basket. Suppose, for example, that despite all our best intentions, we end up testing knowledge in areas that turn out to be unimportant and ignore areas that are extremely important. A national exam ensures that we do this for the whole nation for good or bad. Given the fact that views on education change over time, it is dangerous to induce an entire country to acquire knowledge in one specific body of material.

Technology

With the coming of the information age, one of the more fashionable suggestions is to introduce technology into the schools. Many districts have already funded Internet connections in the classroom, and others have applied for grants and assistance to make an electronic educational environment feasible. Although it is difficult to argue that additional resources do not have some value, the evidence on technology has been, at best, weak, and more often negative.[3] Although the details of why technology can also have a perverse effect on academic achievement are not yet known, some have suggested that technology acts as a substitute rather than a complement to more traditional methods of learning.

One nice feature of introducing technology into the classroom is that it may assist in maintaining the student's attention span. The big negative is that students may spend their time in chat rooms on the Internet rather than working more traditional math problems with pencil and paper. Given our current state of knowledge, it is difficult to argue that a great deal of public money should be spent on introducing technology into the classroom.

My own personal experience as a teacher for over twenty-seven years backs this up. I find that instruction using the blackboard is far more effective than that using overhead transparencies or even slick PowerPoint presentations. Writing on the blackboard is a signal to students that a point is particularly relevant, and it constrains the instructor to present the material at a rate closer to that at which students can absorb the material. An overhead or slide presentation often offers too much information in one short interval and, by overwhelming the students, ends up putting them to sleep.

Accountability

Few policy makers, including those who are part of the education community, would actually argue against accountability. The main problem, however, is defining appropriate standards for accountability and knowing which factors to take into account.

Suppose that we ignore the arguments of the previous section and simply institute a uniform test against which schools are compared. A number of problems remain. First, schools that have students from wealthier and more educated homes are likely to obtain higher test scores even if the school in question is contributing no more to a child's education than other schools in the sample. In other words, demographic characteristics of the student population are likely to have significant effects on test scores. Presumably, society is interested in added value associated with education and not merely a certification that schools have been able to attract a bright group of entrants. Local to the Hoover Institution, Palo Alto schools are known for the high test scores of their students. Is this because the schools are doing a good job, or is it because a large proportion of the students are the children of Stanford faculty or other professionals?

Second, some schools have more resources to work with than others. It is unreasonable to expect that schools operating on a per-student budget that is half that of other schools will be able to produce the same quality of educational output. Going back to the previous argument if nothing else, it will be much more difficult to attract quality teachers on a smaller budget than one that allows higher teacher wages to be paid. The richest districts will have the ability to cherry pick among teacher applicants.

As a potential solution, it is possible to look at gains in scores. A district that has the good fortune to have high-achieving students and/or deep pockets can be asked to make the same percentage gains in achievement as those of poorer or less-well-positioned schools. Thus, a school with an initial average test score of 600 would be required to move its students to 660, while a school that had initial test scores of 500 would be required to move its students to 550. Although something along these lines sounds fair, it penalizes schools that have done well in the past. For example, consider a school that has done the best possible job for its students. As a result, test scores are high, students are happy, and graduation rates are among the highest in the nation. It may be very difficult to add to its stellar record, simply because all the appropriate steps have already been taken. Such schools would be penalized by a system that looked for change rather than levels of performance.

What, then, is the solution? Conceptually, it is necessary to hold demographic characteristics of the student body and resources available to the schools constant. This requires comparisons among similarly situated schools. Although it is straightforward to do this statistically, there remains one major problem. The differences that one observes in test scores across schools are as likely to reflect unobserved differences in school or student characteristics as they are to reflect differences in the actual performance of the school itself. For example, in comparing a school in one part of a wealthy town to another part of that wealthy town, the differences in the test scores obtained by the students are likely to be small. Those small differences may reflect differential performance of the two schools, or small differences in the characteristics of the students who live in different parts of the town. Thus, accountability, although important, is not easily implemented. It can be an important part of the policy equation, but it must be implemented by those who have a sophisticated knowledge of statistical methods as well as educational practices.

One way around the problem is to allow more choice for students. This does not necessarily require private schools, but allowing mobility between schools would provide good signals of how well a school is actually performing. If students tend to move from School A to School B, then one can conclude that students feel that they get more out of School B than School A. Although it is still possible that other factors are involved, this is probably the best indicator that School B is doing a better job than School A in educating students.

HOW SHALL WE DEFINE OUTPUT?

There are a number of ways to measure the performance of a school. The most frequently used measure is student test scores, but many others have been referred to in the past. Literacy rates among students of a certain grade level, high school completion rates, and the proportion going on to college are all indicators of student achievement, but they indicate different things. The measure of output chosen can affect whether a school is viewed as good or bad and can also affect the strategies adopted by a particular school.

Suppose that a school is judged on literacy among its eighth grade school population. That school will attempt to get every child to some basic level of reading, but it will not focus on helping particular students excel in reading. Nor does the school have strong incentives to focus on mathematical skills, because they are not measured by the standard literacy tests.

Suppose instead that we judge a school or school district by the proportion of students who graduate from high school. This would cause the school to focus on those students right on the margin between staying and dropping out.

The poorest students would be ignored because they are unlikely to be swayed into remaining in school by policies that
a school could implement. The best students would also be
likely to be ignored because they are not at a high risk of
dropping out. As a result, schools target a particular part of
the student population, in this case at the low, but not the
lowest, part of the achievement distribution.

At the other extreme, one can imagine basing an assessment of school performance on the proportion of students
who go on to college, or even on those who go on to elite
colleges. Such an output measure would influence schools to
focus on the better students in the class, perhaps to the disadvantage of those in the middle or bottom of the class.

Another measure of school performance looks at the bottom line: how do schools affect subsequent earnings or the
occupational distribution of their students? For many purposes, this is exactly the right measure of school performance. The problem with this measure is that it is very
difficult to obtain, and even when possible, it comes only
after a very long lag. By the time the students have earnings
to report, the school may have already changed its policies
many times over.

OTHER POLICIES

A number of state governors have suggested policies that
might help make their schools more effective. Most involve
some subsidy or transfer program.

Some have suggested that more money be given to schools
so that they can create advanced placement classes in schools
that primarily teach disadvantaged children. Although this
may be a nice addition to such schools, we return to the issues discussed in the previous section. Are we more concerned about bringing the middle students up to the top, or
about bringing the bottom up to the middle? My sense is
that it is the latter, and this sense is backed up by statistics
on high school dropout rates. In disadvantaged schools in

low-income and minority areas, dropout rates are extremely high, suggesting that the target probably should be basic literacy skills and high school graduation rather than college placement.

Another suggestion is to give bonuses and forgivable loans to teachers who agree to teach in currently poorly performing schools. The issue here is whether this simply serves to shift teachers around or actually recruits more able individuals into the teaching profession. If the policy only shifts teachers around, then it is hardly clear that moving teachers who were effective in good schools to schools with much more poorly performing students will actually improve educational output. Even if it does so for the disadvantaged students, one has to ask what the effects will be on the students that they have left behind. To the extent that such policy actually improves the quality of individuals entering teaching, it is probably a worthwhile social investment. The problem is that the amount of time it takes for such a policy to work is significant, and it is far from obvious that the inducement into teaching will be large unless the bonuses are themselves quite large.

Other policies provide for college assistance to middle- and low-income families. This is a politically attractive policy, but it does not target the problem. There is little evidence to support the view that too few people go to college. The private rates of return to college are high but commensurate with other investments that have similar risk. Furthermore, college students seem to capture most of the return to their investments in their own college education in the form of higher earnings, which suggests that there is not a great necessity to help out at this end. Obviously, there are some students who are precluded from going to college because of the inability to raise resources. This is a small problem, however, relative to the one that plagues those who never get to the college level at all. Once again, moving the students who are at the bottom to the middle is probably a more important social goal than moving those in the middle to the upper middle.

CONCLUSION

This book covers a large number of issues. Education is a complicated but important topic. It is our hope that the essays included here will shed light on what education does, on various ways to structure education, and on lessons that can be learned from the past, as well as help us understand how much can be accomplished in the future.

NOTES

1. See, for example, Eric A. Hanushek, "Conclusions and Controversies about the Effectiveness of School Resources," *Economic Policy Review* IV (March 1998b): 11-27. Hanushek finds little evidence that anything, including class size reductions, matters. See also James Coleman and Thomas Hoffer, *Public and Private Schools: The Impact on Communities* (New York: Basic Books, 1987) and James Coleman, Sally Kilgore, and Thomas Hoffer, *Public and Private High Schools* (Washington, D.C.: National Center for Educational Statistics, 1981). These two studies report that Catholic schools with larger class sizes produce better students than public school classes against which they are compared.
2. The argument is spelled out in detail in Edward P. Lazear, "Educational Production," *Quarterly Journal of Economics* (August 2001): 1-27.
3. See Joshua Angrist and Victor Lavy, "New Evidence on Classroom Computers and Pupil Learning" (NBER Working Paper 7424, November 1999).

Education and Income

The Age of Human Capital

Gary S. Becker

THE AGE OF HUMAN CAPITAL

Human capital refers to the knowledge, information, ideas, skills, and health of individuals. This is the "age of human capital" in the sense that human capital is by far the most important form of capital in modern economies. The economic successes of individuals, and also of whole economies, depends on how extensively and effectively people invest in themselves.

Studies suggest that capital invested in men and women constitutes over 70 percent of the total capital in the United States. The total invested in schooling, on-the-job training, health, information, and research and development is surely over 20 percent of gross domestic product. Technology may be the driver of a modern economy, especially of its high-tech sector, but human capital is certainly the fuel.

An economy like that of the United States is called a capitalist economy, but a more accurate term is *human* capital or a *knowledge* capital economy. While all forms of capital are important, including machinery, factories, and financial capital, human capital is the most significant.

STOCK MARKET CRASHES AND HUMAN CAPITAL

More than a decade ago, I used the significance of human capital to make one of my more useful short-term business forecasts. You may recall that on October 17, 1987—so-called Black Monday—the value of the stocks listed on the New York Stock Exchange fell by 22 percent. On one day alone, equity wealth declined 22 percent. There was chaos in Washington and in the media. Financial magazines were predicting another Great Recession like the one in 1929, when the stock market also crashed.

I happened to be working on my regular monthly *Business Week* column during the day of the 1987 crash. So on Black Monday, I scrapped the column I was preparing and wrote one that predicted no major recession for the United States. This column ran about the same time as an issue of *Business Week* in which the cover story focused on a possible major depression due to the crash.

My argument was very simple. I began by emphasizing that human capital is three-fourths, or so, of the wealth in the United States, and that the value of human capital did not seem to have been much affected by the stock market crash. It is known that financial returns and human capital returns generally vary largely independently of each other. If so, the crash would only affect the value of the nonhuman capital, a fraction of all wealth. By multiplying the fraction of wealth that crashed in value by the size of the fall, I showed that the total wealth of the economy declined by only a few percentage points, perhaps as little as two percent. That could cause trouble, but not by itself a major recession. This is why I predicted difficult times only for luxury goods and the like—which did happen. Three months after the crash, the economy was back on course, and quarterly time series on stock prices show little evidence of the crash.

THE GROWING RETURN TO HUMAN CAPITAL

The modern economic environment places more of a premium on education, training, and other sources of knowledge than was true even fifty years ago. This can be inferred from changes in the relation between education and earnings. In the United States during most of the past forty years, college graduates earned on the average about 50 percent more than high school graduates, and the latter earned about 30 percent more than high school dropouts. (See Figure 1 for the college–high school earnings gap.)

Wage differences between typical college and high school graduates increased from 40 percent in 1977 to 60 percent in the 1990s. The gap between high school graduates and persons with at least a college education grew even faster, from 50 percent in the late 1960s to about 75 percent in recent years. These are probably the largest increases in U.S. history.

Similar trends are found elsewhere toward greater demand for more skilled workers, although in Europe this has taken the form of increased unemployment of less educated and less trained workers. The gap in wage differentials by education is large in European nations for both men and women.

The global economy cannot succeed without considerable investment in human capital by all nations. Richer countries specialize in high-knowledge products and services, while poorer nations specialize in lower-skilled and raw material–intensive products. Still, investments in human capital are also necessary in poorer nations if they are to have a chance of growing out of poverty.

Almost without exception, studies of the economic growth of different nations show a close relation during the past several decades between economic performance and schooling, life expectancy, and other human capital measures. In particular, although on the average Third World nations grew a little less rapidly than richer ones, poorer nations with more educated and healthier populations managed to grow faster than average. Especially important for these nations are their investments in elementary and secondary education.

Of course, machines and other physical capital are important. But alone they are far from sufficient to produce growth because skilled workers and managers, and innovative entrepreneurs, are needed to operate complicated machinery, to

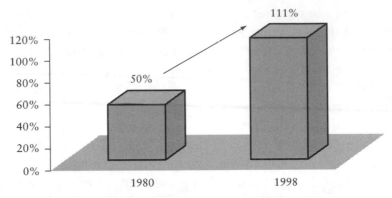

FIGURE 1. Widening Pay-Gap Between High School and
   College Graduates
(SOURCE: 1980: U.S. Census Bureau. 1999: ML Growth Stock Research)

produce efficiently, to develop new products and processes, and to utilize innovations from other countries. Neglect of human capital and world markets by most economists after World War II, and their emphasis on import substitution and protected markets, was a seriously distorted view of the growth process. Ultimately it was a failed vision of what is essential to achieve economic progress and reductions in poverty.

DISTANCE LEARNING

Modern economies require that people invest in the acquisition of knowledge, skills, and information not only when young but throughout most of their lives. Yet the basic methods of acquiring human capital have hardly changed since the time of Socrates. For 2,500 years, teachers and students have met face to face for lectures and discussions. However, the growth of the Internet will revolutionize the system of teaching and learning by allowing "distance learning," where teachers and students may interact closely even though they are separated physically and in time.

The key economic advantage of distance learning over traditional on-site learning is that it saves students time.

Studies show that the value of time spent learning is the principal cost of investment in human capital among teenagers and adults with even moderate actual or potential earnings. It is especially important for executives and highly skilled employees. Web-based instruction eliminates regular commutes to schools and other teaching facilities, which can amount to more than an hour each way for persons with jobs. On-line instruction also allows greater time flexibility for students to interact with course materials, "chat" with other students, take quizzes, and submit reports. People with full-time jobs can choose the most convenient time to do their coursework, including during weekends, before work, and after.

Thousands of Internet students could take a single, popular course, instead of the small numbers in a typical classroom. The spread of faster and, ultimately, broadband access to the Web enables the use of colorful graphics and attractive simulations. On-line instruction may well widen the market and raise the popularity of superstar teachers who command high audiences and very high salaries.

Distance learning appeals mainly to adults who want to take courses toward a bachelor's or master's degree or maintain and upgrade job skills that have grown outdated. Highly skilled professionals, such as doctors, have always had to keep up with change in their fields by reading and by taking short courses. But the continual introduction of new technologies makes skills obsolescence a serious prospect for all professionals and for many other working adults.

On-the-job training and learning offer a particularly promising on-line market. Companies have long invested in employee education, although mostly in-house to eliminate travel time to off-site schools. Distance learning offers an opportunity to outsource teaching to specialized companies without taking employees away from their work. Web-based courses are rapidly developing in information technology, finance, accounting, marketing, management, the global economy, and many other subject areas.

How well companies manage their human capital is a crucial factor in their success. Bill Gates said, "Take our 20 best people away and . . . Microsoft would become an unimportant company."

Unfortunately, the huge amounts invested by companies are not on their balance sheets because typically they are costed as current spending rather than capitalized. They are part of "goodwill" and other residual accounting categories. Increased investments in human capital and knowledge by companies partly explains the enormous rise in the ratio of market price to book value of the assets of publically traded companies.

CONCLUSIONS

I conclude by listing several main points of this essay:

1. Human capital is of great importance in the modern economy.

2. Human capital has become of much greater significance during the past two decades.

3. Human capital is crucial to the international division of labor.

4. Much unmeasured learning goes on in companies and by adults.

5. People need to invest in themselves during their whole lives.

6. Distance learning will become of crucial importance to the teaching and learning process.

7. Human capital stimulates technological innovations and the high-tech sector.

Education as a Determinant of Economic Growth

Robert J. Barro

Since the late 1980s, much of the attention of macroeconomists has focused on long-term issues, notably the effects of government policies on the long-run rate of economic growth. This emphasis reflects the recognition that the difference between prosperity and poverty for a country depends on how fast it grows over the long term. Although standard macroeconomic policies are important for growth, other aspects of "policy"—broadly interpreted to encompass all government activities that matter for economic performance—are even more significant.

This paper focuses on human capital as a determinant of economic growth. Although human capital includes education, health, and aspects of "social capital," the focus of the present study is on education. The analysis stresses the distinction between the quantity of education—measured by years of attainment at various levels—and the quality, gauged by scores on internationally comparable examinations.

The recognition that the determination of long-term economic growth was the central macroeconomic problem was fortunately accompanied in the late 1980s by important advances in the theory of economic growth. This period featured the development of models in which purposeful research and application led over time to new and better products and methods of production. Also central to the analysis was the manner in which technological advances in leading countries were imitated and adapted in less developed countries. The key feature of these frameworks was that the long-term rate of economic growth was explained within the model. For that reason, the line of research became known by the perhaps inelegant term endogenous growth theory. (In fact, the phrase received sufficient popular attention in the mid 1990s that it was inadvertently referred to as "indigenous growth theory" in the British press by the then Chancellor of the Exchequer, Kenneth Clarke.)

Shortly thereafter, in the early 1990s, there was a good deal of empirical estimation of growth models using cross-country and cross-regional data. This empirical work was, in some sense, inspired by the excitement of the new growth theories. However, the framework for the applied work owed more to an older type of growth theory, called the neoclassical growth model, which economists developed in the 1950s and 1960s. A central element of this analysis is the diminishing returns to the accumulation of physical capital. This property produces a convergence force whereby poor economies tend to catch up to rich ones. The main reason for convergence is the tendency for countries to experience diminishing returns as they get richer. However, this tendency is affected by various dimensions of government policy and by the accumulation of human capital. Therefore, the framework used in recent empirical studies has incorporated these additional factors.

The recent endogenous-growth models are useful for understanding why advanced economies—and the world as a whole—can continue to grow in the long run despite the tendency for diminishing returns in the accumulation of physical and human capital. In contrast, the older, neoclassical growth model does well for understanding relative growth rates across countries, for example, for assessing why South Korea grew much faster than the United States or Zaire over the last thirty years. Thus, overall, the new and old theories are more complementary than they are competing.

EMPIRICAL FINDINGS ON GROWTH AND INVESTMENT ACROSS COUNTRIES

Empirical Framework

My empirical findings on economic growth, described in an earlier form in Barro,[1] provide estimates for the effects of a number of government policies and other variables. The analysis applies to roughly one hundred countries observed from 1960 to 1995.

The framework includes countries at vastly different levels of economic development, and places are excluded only because of missing data. The attractive feature of this broad sample is that it encompasses great variation in the policies and other variables that are to be evaluated. In fact, my view is that it is impossible to use the experience of one or a few countries to accurately assess the long-term growth effects from legal and educational institutions, size of government, monetary and fiscal policies, and other variables.

One challenge in the broad cross-country study is to measure variables in a consistent and accurate way across countries and over time. Less developed countries tend, in particular, to have a lot of measurement error in national accounts and other data. Given this problem, the use of the broad panel relies on the idea that the strong signal from the diversity of the experience dominates the noise.

The empirical work considers average growth rates of per capita gross domestic product (GDP) over three ten-year periods, 1965–75, 1975–85, and 1985–95. In one respect, this long-term context is forced by the data, because many of the variables considered, including school attainment, are measured at best over five-year intervals. Data on internationally comparable test scores are available for even fewer years. The low-frequency context accords, in any event, with the underlying theories of growth, which attempt to explain long-term growth, not short-run business fluctuations.

The empirical results relate the rate of economic growth to the initial standard of living, measured by the level of GDP, and to a set of other explanatory variables. The other variables include an array of policy measures: the ratio of government consumption outlays to GDP, a subjective indicator of the maintenance of the rule of law, a measure of international openness (the ratio of exports plus imports to GDP), and the inflation rate (based on consumer price indexes). Also included are the total fertility rate (a prime determinant of population growth), the ratio of investment to GDP, and the growth rate of the terms of trade (export prices relative to import prices).

Education Data

The main education variable is one that I found previously had significant explanatory power for economic growth. This variable is the value at the start of each period of the average years of school attainment at the upper (secondary and tertiary) levels for males aged 25 and over. The analysis also considers several alternative measures of the quantity and quality of education: primary school attainment, attainment by females, and results on internationally comparable examinations.

The construction of the school-attainment data is discussed in Barro and Lee.[2a, 2b] The basic procedure was to begin with census figures on educational attainment. These data were compiled primarily by the United Nations, based on information from individual countries. Missing observations were filled in by using school-enrollment data. Effectively, enrollment is the investment flow that connects the stock of attainment to subsequent stocks. The resulting data set includes information for most countries on school attainment at various levels over five-year intervals from 1960 to 1990. The data set has recently been revised and updated; see Barro and Lee[3] for details. The new information includes actual figures for 1995 and projections to 2000.

Basic Empirical Results

Before focusing on the results for education, it is worthwhile to provide a quick summary of the results for the other explanatory variables.

The level of per-capita GDP.   As is now well known, the simple relation across countries between growth rates and initial levels of per capita GDP is virtually zero. However, this relation is misleading, because richer countries tend to have more favorable values of the other explanatory variables, such as rule of law and educational attainment. It is possible statistically to hold these other effects constant, that is, to assess the effect on economic growth from a change in the starting level of per capita GDP for given values of the other explanatory variables. When we do this, we isolate a strong, inverse relation between growth rate and level.

The estimates imply the relation between the growth rate and initial level of per capita GDP as shown in Figure 1.[4] This relation is negative overall but is not linear. For the poorest countries in the sample, the marginal effect of the starting level of per capita GDP on the growth rate is small and may even be positive. The estimates imply a positive effect for a level of per capita GDP less than $580 (in 1985 prices). This situation applies mainly to some countries in sub-Saharan Africa.

For the richest countries, the effect of the initial level of per capita GDP on the growth rate is strongly negative. The largest magnitude (corresponding to the highest value of per capita GDP in 1995) is for Luxembourg—the GDP value of $19,794 implies an effect of –0.059 on the growth rate. The United States has the next largest value of GDP in 1995 ($18,951), implying an estimated effect on the growth rate of –0.058. These values mean that an increase in per capita GDP of 10 percent implies a decrease in the growth rate on impact by 0.6 percent per year. However, an offsetting force, already noted, is that higher levels of per capita GDP tend to be associated with more favorable values of other explanatory variables, such as more schooling, lower fertility, and better maintenance of the rule of law. That is why richer countries perform reasonably well in terms of observed rates of economic growth.

Overall, the cross-country evidence shows no pattern of absolute convergence—whereby poor countries tend systematically to grow faster than rich ones—but does provide strong

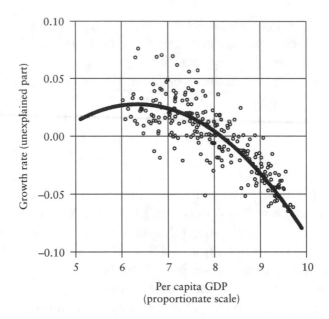

FIGURE 1. Growth Rate versus GDP.

evidence of conditional convergence. That is, except possibly at extremely low levels of per capita product, a poorer country tends to grow faster for given values of the policy and other explanatory variables. The pattern of absolute convergence does not appear because poor countries tend systematically to have less favorable values of the explanatory variables.

Government consumption.   The ratio of government consumption to GDP is intended to measure a set of public outlays that do not directly enhance an economy's productivity. In interpreting the estimated effect on growth, it is important to note that measures of taxation are not being held constant. This omission reflects data problems in constructing accurate representations for various tax rates, such as marginal rates on labor and capital income, and so on. Since the tax side has not been held constant, the effect of a higher government consumption ratio on growth involves partly a direct impact and partly an indirect effect involving the required increase in overall public revenues.

The results indicate that the effect of the government consumption ratio on economic growth is significantly negative. An increase in the ratio by 10 percentage points is estimated to reduce the growth rate on impact by 1.6 percent per year.

The rule of law.   Many analysts believe that secure property rights and a strong legal system are central for investment and other aspects of economic activity.[5] The empirical challenge has been to measure these concepts in a reliable way across countries and over time. Probably the best indicators available come from international consulting firms that advise clients on the attractiveness of countries as places for investments. These investors are concerned about institutional matters such as the prevalence of law and order, the capacity of the legal system to enforce contracts, the efficiency of the bureaucracy, the likelihood of government expropriation, and the extent of official corruption. These kinds of factors have been assessed by a number of consulting companies, including Political Risk Services in its publication *International Country Risk Guide*.[6] This source is especially useful because it covers over one hundred countries since the early 1980s. Although the data are subjective, they have the virtue of being prepared contemporaneously by local experts.

Among the various indicators available, the index for overall maintenance of the rule of law (also referred to as "law and order tradition") turns out to have the most explanatory power for economic growth. This index was initially measured by Political Risk Services in seven categories on a zero-to-six scale, with six the most favorable. The index has been converted here to a zero-to-one scale, with zero indicating the poorest maintenance of the rule of law and one the best.

The results indicate that increased maintenance of the rule of law has a positive and statistically significant effect on the rate of economic growth. An improvement by one category among the seven used by Political Risk Services (that is, an increase in the zero-to-one index by 0.17) is estimated to raise the growth rate on impact by 0.2 percent per year.

International openness.   Openness to international trade is often thought to be conducive to economic growth. The basic measure of openness used here is the ratio of exports plus imports to GDP. The results show that the openness variable has a significantly positive effect on growth. However, there is some indication that the effect on growth diminishes as a country gets richer. The estimates imply that the influence of openness on growth would reach zero at a per capita GDP of $11,700 (1985 U.S. dollars). This value is below the per capita GDP of the richest countries, such as the United States. Hence, it may well be true that the NAFTA treaty promoted growth in Mexico but not in the United States and Canada.

The inflation rate.   The results show a marginally significant, negative effect of inflation on the rate of economic growth. The estimates imply that an increase in the average rate of inflation by 10 percent per year would lower the growth rate on impact by 0.14 percent per year.

The fertility rate.   The results indicate that economic growth is significantly negatively related to the total fertility rate. Thus, the choice to have more children per adult—and, hence, in the long run, to have a higher rate of population growth—comes at the expense of growth in output per person.

The investment ratio.   The estimates indicate that the growth rate depends positively and marginally significantly on the investment ratio. This effect applies for given values of policy and other variables, as already discussed, which also turn out to affect the investment ratio. For example, an improvement in the rule of law raises investment and also raises growth for a given amount of investment.

The terms of trade. The results show that improvements in the terms of trade (a higher growth rate of the ratio of export prices to import prices) enhance economic growth.

Effects of Education

Governments typically have strong direct involvement in the financing and provision of schooling at various levels. Hence, public policies in these areas have major effects on a country's accumulation of human capital. One measure of this schooling capital is the average years of attainment, as discussed before. These data are classified by sex and age (for persons aged 15 and over and 25 and over) and by levels of education (no school, partial and complete primary, partial and complete secondary, and partial and complete higher).

For a given level of initial per capita GDP, a higher initial stock of human capital signifies a higher ratio of human to physical capital. This higher ratio tends to generate higher economic growth through at least two channels. First, more human capital facilitates the absorption of superior technologies from leading countries. This channel is likely to be especially important for schooling at the secondary and higher levels. Second, human capital tends to be more difficult to adjust than physical capital. Therefore, a country that starts with a high ratio of human to physical capital—such as in the aftermath of a war that destroys primarily physical capital—tends to grow rapidly by adjusting upward the quantity of physical capital.

Years of schooling. The empirical results indicate that the average years of school attainment at the secondary and higher levels for males aged 25 and over has a positive and significant effect on the subsequent rate of economic growth.[7] Figure 2 depicts this relationship. The estimates imply that an additional year of schooling (roughly a one-standard-deviation change) raises the growth rate on impact by 0.44 percent per year. As already mentioned, a possible interpretation of this effect is that a work force educated at the secondary and higher

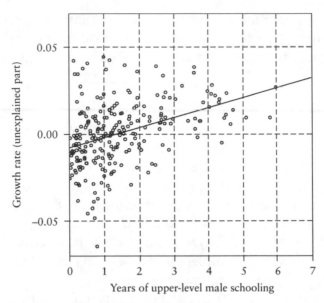

FIGURE 2.   Growth Rate versus Schooling

levels facilitates the absorption of technologies from more advanced foreign countries.

The implied social rate of return on schooling—that is, the rate of return to the overall economy—is complicated. First, the system already holds fixed the level of per capita GDP and, therefore, does not pick up a contemporaneous effect of schooling on output. Rather, the effect from an additional year of average school attainment impacts on the growth rate of GDP and thereby affects the level of GDP gradually over time. Because of the convergence force—whereby higher levels of GDP feed back negatively into the growth rate—the ultimate effect of more schooling on the level of output (relative to a fixed trend) is finite.

Suppose that the convergence rate—the negative effect of higher per capita GDP on the growth rate—is 2.5 percent per year, which is the average value estimated across countries. In this case, the estimated effect of the schooling variable on growth turns out to imply that an additional year of attainment for the typical adult raises the level of output asymptotically by 19 percent. This figure would give the implied social real rate of return to education (for males at the secondary and higher levels) if the cost of an individual's additional year of schooling equaled one year of foregone per capita GDP, if there were no depreciation in stocks of schooling capital (due, for example, to aging and mortality), and if the adjustment to the 19 percent higher level of output occurred with no lag. The finiteness of the convergence rate and the presence of depreciation imply lower rates of return. However, an opposing force is that the cost of an added year of schooling is probably less than one year's per capita GDP, because the cost of students' time spent at school would be less than the economy's average wage rate. We must, however, also consider the costs of teachers' time and other school inputs. In any event, if we neglect depreciation and assume that the cost of an additional year of schooling equals one year's foregone per capita GDP, then a convergence rate of 2.5 percent per year turns out to imply a social rate of return to schooling of 7 percent per year. This figure is within the range of typical microeconomic estimates of returns to education.

The empirical analysis has also considered additional dimensions of the years of schooling. Female attainment at the secondary and higher levels turns out not to have significant explanatory power for economic growth. One possible explanation for the weak role of female upper-level schooling as a determinant of growth is that many countries follow discriminatory practices that prevent the efficient exploitation of well-educated females in the formal labor market. Given these practices, it is not surprising that more resources devoted to upper-level female education would not show up as enhanced growth.

Male primary schooling turns out not to have significant explanatory power for growth, whereas female primary schooling has a positive, but statistically insignificant, effect. The particular importance of schooling at the secondary and higher levels (for males) supports the idea that education affects growth by facilitating the absorption of new technologies—which are likely to be complementary with labor educated to these higher levels. Primary schooling is, however, critical as a prerequisite for secondary education.

Another role for primary schooling involves the well-known negative effect of female primary education on fertility rates. However, the female primary attainment variable would not be credited with this growth effect, because the fertility variable is included separately in the system that was estimated. If fertility is not included, then the estimated growth effect of female primary schooling becomes significantly positive.

Quality of education. Many researchers argue that the quality of schooling is more important than the quantity, measured, for example, by years of attainment. Barro and Lee[8] discuss the available cross-country aggregate measures of the quality of education. Hanushek and Kim[9] find that scores on international examinations—indicators of the quality of schooling—matter more than years of attainment for subsequent economic growth. My findings turn out to accord with their results.

Information on student test scores—for science, mathematics, and reading—is available for forty-three countries in the sample, that is, for about half of the countries. The available data were used to construct a single cross section of test scores on the science, reading, and mathematics examinations.[10] These variables were then entered into the systems for economic growth that I considered before.

The first result is that science scores have a significantly positive effect on economic growth. With science scores included, the estimated effect of male upper-level attainment is still positive but only weakly statistically significant. The estimated effect implies that a one-standard-deviation increase in science test scores—by 0.08—would raise the growth rate on impact by 1.0 percent per year. In contrast, the estimated effect of the school attainment variable now implies that a one-standard-deviation rise in attainment would increase the growth rate on impact by only 0.2 percent per year. Thus, the results suggest that the quality and quantity of schooling both matter for growth but that quality is much more important.

Given the findings, it would be of considerable interest for a country to know how to improve the quality of education, as reflected in test scores. The results presented in Barro and Lee (1998) indicate that test scores are positively related to the average school attainment of adults (which would reflect parents' education) and negatively related to pupil-teacher ratios. Thus, the aggregate data indicate that smaller class sizes have beneficial effects. This relationship is controversial in micro studies. Another finding is that the length of the school term was unrelated to the test scores. In addition, pupils from Asian countries performed unusually well on the tests.

Many microeconomic studies have found that test scores may just proxy for other characteristics of students, such as family income and parents' education. Therefore, it is difficult to tell whether a positive relation between test scores and student outcomes, such as future earnings, reflects the quality of education or these other characteristics. In my cross-country analysis, the effects of test scores (and years of school attainment) apply after taking account of the other explanatory variables, including per capita GDP. Therefore, the estimated effects of schooling quality—as gauged by the test scores—would apply for a given value of per capita GDP and the other variables.

Mathematics scores turn out also to have a positive influence on growth. However, the results indicate that the science scores are somewhat more predictive of economic growth, and it is difficult from the available data to disentangle the effects of these two types of test scores.

There is also a weak indication that reading scores have a positive effect on economic growth. However, it is again difficult with the available data to separate this effect from those of science and mathematics scores.

Finally, as an attempt to increase the sample size, I constructed a single test-scores variable that was based on science scores, where available, and then filled in some missing observations by using the reading scores.[11] The results, now for

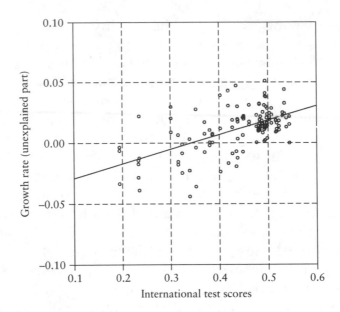

FIGURE 3. Growth Rate versus Test Scores

a somewhat larger sample, again indicate a significantly positive effect on growth. Figure 3 shows graphically the relation between economic growth and the overall test-scores variable. The Figure makes clear that test scores have strong explanatory power for economic growth.

SUMMARY OF MAJOR RESULTS

The determinants of economic growth were analyzed for around one hundred countries observed from 1960 to 1995. The data reveal a pattern of conditional convergence in the sense that the growth rate of per capita GDP is inversely related to the starting level of per capita GDP. Other variables that influenced economic growth included measures of government policies and institutions, initial stocks of human capital, and the character of the national population.

With respect to education, growth is positively related to the starting level of average years of school attainment of adult males at the secondary and higher levels. Since workers with this educational background would be complementary with new technologies, the results suggest an important role for the diffusion of technology in the development process. Growth is insignificantly related to years of school attainment of females at the secondary and higher levels. This result suggests that highly educated women are not well utilized in the labor markets of many countries. Growth is insignificantly related to male schooling at the primary level. However, this level of schooling is a prerequisite for secondary schooling and would therefore affect growth through this channel. Education of women at the primary level stimulates economic growth indirectly by inducing a lower fertility rate.

Data on students' scores on internationally comparable examinations in science, mathematics, and reading were used to measure the quality of schooling. Scores on science tests have a particularly strong positive relation with economic growth. Given the quality of education, as represented by the test scores, the quantity of schooling—measured by average years of attainment of adult males at the secondary and higher levels—is still positively related to subsequent growth. However, the effect of school quality is quantitatively much more important.

NOTES

1. Robert J. Barro, *Determinants of Economic Growth: A Cross-Country Empirical Study* (Cambridge, Mass.: MIT Press, 1997).
2a. Robert J. Barro and Jong-Wha Lee, "International Comparisons of Educational Attainment," *Journal of Monetary Economics* 32 (1993): 363–94.
2b. Robert J. Barro and Jong-Wha Lee, "International Measures of Schooling Years and Schooling Quality," *American Economic Review* 86 (1996): 218–23.
3. Robert J. Barro and Jong-Wha Lee, "International Data on Educational Attainment Updates and Implications," unpublished, Harvard University, January 2000, forthcoming in *Oxford Economic Papers*.

4. The variable plotted on the vertical axis is the growth rate net of the estimated effect of all the explanatory variables aside from the initial value of per capita GDP. The construction in the two subsequent figures is analogous. The horizontal axis uses a proportionate scale.

5. In previous analyses, I also looked for effects of democracy, measured either by political rights or civil liberties. Results using subjective data from Freedom House indicated that these measures had little explanatory power for economic growth, once the rule-of-law indicator and the other explanatory variables were held constant. Raymond D. Gastil, *Freedom in the World* (Westport, Conn.: Greenwood Press, 1982–83 and other years). Recent editions are published by Freedom House.

6. These data were introduced to economists by Stephen Knack and Philip Keefer, "Institutions and Economic Performance: Cross-Country Tests Using Alternative Institutional Measures," *Economics and Politics* 7 (1995): 207–27. Two other consulting services that construct these type of data are Business Environmental Risk Intelligence (BERI) and Business International, now a part of the Economist Intelligence Unit.

7. The results are basically the same if the years of attainment apply to males aged 15 and over.

8. Robert J. Barro and Jong-Wha Lee, "Determinants of Schooling Quality," unpublished, Harvard University, July 1998, forthcoming in *Economica*.

9. Eric Hanushek and Dongwook Kim, "Schooling, Labor Force Quality, and the Growth of Nations" unpublished, University of Rochester (1999).

10. The data, measured as percent correct on each exam, apply to students, not to current participants in the labor force. More recently, the International Adult Literacy Survey provided test results for the working-age population. However, these data are at an early stage and cover only a few OECD countries—see OECD. *Human Capital Investment—An International Comparison*, OECD (Organization for Economic Cooperation and Development), Paris (1998) for a discussion.

11. The mathematics scores turned out not to provide any additional observations.

The Value of Education: Evidence from Around the Globe

Robert E. Hall

In the United States education is a worthwhile investment. College graduates earn substantially more than high-school graduates, who earn more in turn than dropouts. Figure 1 shows recent U.S. data on annual earnings by education. It is worth almost $18,000 per year over what the holder of a B.A. earns to hold a graduate or professional degree. The college graduate earns, on the average, about $20,000 annually more than a high school graduate, and the benefit to graduating from high school rather than dropping out is about $8,000 per year in earnings. These figures understate the true differentials because they do not include the extra fringe benefits that go with higher earnings.

What about the rest of the world? Does education raise personal earnings in other industrial countries? In mid-level developing countries such as Turkey or Brazil? In the Third World countries of Africa and south Asia? Research has shown a strong relation between education and earnings in virtually every country studied. The percentage increase in earnings from an additional year of education is higher in countries with lower general levels of education. A recent survey shows that the additional year adds 13.4 percent to earnings in sub-Sahara Africa, 10.1 percent in

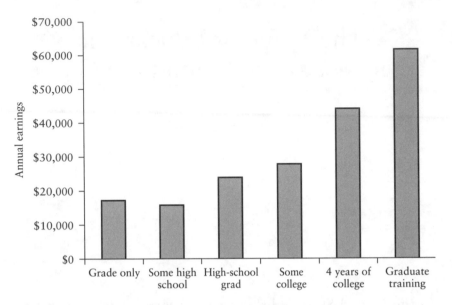

FIGURE 1.   Annual Earnings of U.S. Workers by Education, 1998

(SOURCE: U.S. Bureau of the Census, Current Population Survey)

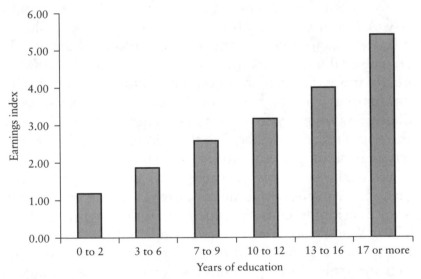

FIGURE 2.   How Education Contributes to an Individual's Earnings
(Based on Worldwide Data)

(SOURCE: Robert E. Hall and Charles I. Jones, "Why Do Some Countries Produce So
Much More Output per Worker Than Others?" *Quarterly Journal of Economics* 114
[February 1999]: 83–116.)

the average country, and 6.8 percent in the well-educated countries making up the Organization for Economic Co-operation and Development (OECD) (United States, Japan, and Western Europe).[1] Figure 2 shows the relationship in a format similar to Figure 1. The figure shows an index of earnings by education level. The levels on the horizontal axis include categories not shown for the United States, where very few workers have less than a high school education.

The data show conclusively that education matters for the individual. A young person enjoys a substantially higher lifetime income for a few years' investment in education, even in countries where conditions seem unfavorable and the quality of education is generally low.

Some observers are concerned that education may pay off to the individual but not to the nation. For example, college graduates in Third World countries may find employment mainly in government bureaucracies. To deal with that issue, researchers have considered the relation between national average levels of education and productivity. This research has found a strong favorable effect of education.

A good measure of productivity for this purpose is output per worker. A team at the University of Pennsylvania has developed good measures of output for most of the countries of the world.[2] In principle, the data reflect physical measures of output, such as tons of steel or numbers of cars. They are intended to be insulated from distortions associated with exchange rate movements in particular. My own research in collaboration with Charles Jones makes one further adjustment with the data.[3] Some countries, notably oil producers, have high levels of recorded output because they extract natural resources from the ground. To remove this influence, which has little to do with the productivity of workers, we deducted the part of output arising in the mining and petroleum extraction industries. The data refer to the year 1988, before the collapse of the Soviet Union and the reunification of Germany.

Output per worker varies tremendously among the countries of the world, as Figure 3 illustrates. Down the left are

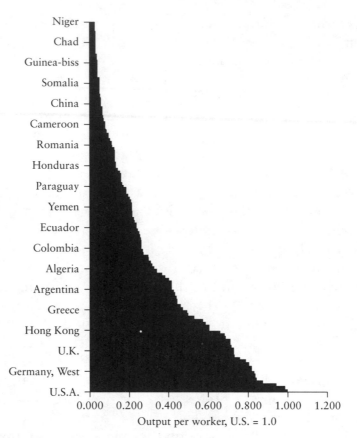

FIGURE 3.   Output per Worker in 127 Countries
(SOURCE: See Figure 2)

examples of countries at each level of output per worker, moving downward in the figure in increasing order. The horizontal position of the gray area measures the output per worker of countries at that level in relation to the United States, the country with the highest output per worker. The countries at the top produce less than one-fortieth the level of the United States.

Jones and I calculated an index of education per worker by taking data on the educational attainment of the population of each country and applying the relative productivity factors from Figure 2. For example, our measure for a hypothetical country where everybody finished college would be about five

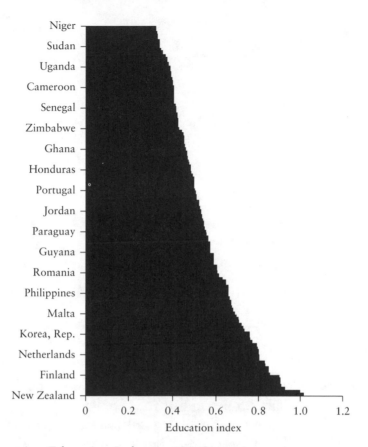

FIGURE 4.   Education Index in 127 Countries
(SOURCE: See Figure 2)

times higher than the measure for a country where everybody attended only first grade. Our measure is appropriate if the differences in earnings do correspond to differences in actual productivity. We stated our index in relation to the U.S. level of education-related productivity. Figure 4 shows the variation among countries in their education indexes in the same format as Figure 3.

There is nowhere near as much variation in education across countries as there is variation in output per worker. I will shortly discuss the other factors that account for low output per worker in countries such as Niger, where the education

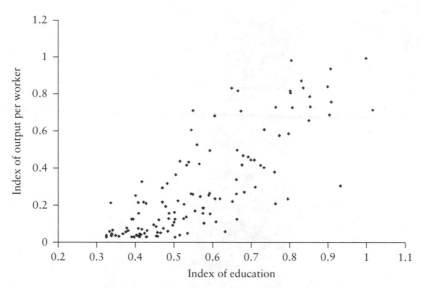

FIGURE 5.   The Relation Between Education and Output per
    Worker Across Countries

(SOURCE: See Figure 2)

index is about 40 percent of the U.S. level, but output per
worker is less than 2.5 percent of the U.S. level.

The education index correlates substantially with output
per worker, as Figure 5 shows. The diamonds mark the value
of the education index by the horizontal position, and output per worker by the vertical position. Those at the lower
left denote the low-output, low-education countries at the
tops of Figures 3 and 4. Those at the upper right are the
high-output, high-education countries. Some countries de-
part from the general pattern. For example, Hungary has an
education index not far below the very top countries, but its
low output per worker is comparable to countries with
much less education, such as Brazil and Iran. Hungary and
other then-Soviet-bloc countries tended to have low levels of
output given their resources.

Figure 5 provides powerful support for the idea that education makes a genuine contribution to productivity and is
not just a credential that raises individuals' earnings. Raising

the general level of education is almost certainly an appropriate top priority for a country aiming to raise its standard of living. But other factors matter for output per worker. One is the amount of plant and equipment available to combine with workers' efforts to produce goods and services. My research with Jones developed a measure of plant and equipment stocks for the countries reported in the previous figures. A second determinant of output per worker is the efficiency of the economy in production. Some countries are more effective in organizing production and are able to achieve higher levels of output from the same amounts of capital, labor, and education as other countries. Jones and I also calculated efficiency indexes for the countries in our sample. We do not have an independent measure of efficiency—we infer efficiency from data on output and inputs.

Table 1 reports the values of the indexes for selected representative countries. In all cases, the United States has the value 1.0—all of the numbers for other countries are stated as ratios to the U.S. level. Although the United States is close to the top in all three determinants—education, plant equipment, and efficiency—it does not rank first in any of them. New Zealand (not shown in Table 1) had slightly more education. The Soviet Union (in 1988) had substantially more plant and equipment in relation to output than did the United States. Italy is well ahead of the United States in terms of efficiency, along with France and Hong Kong. But the United States is sufficiently high in all three components to have the highest result from multiplying the three together, that is, the highest output per worker.

The three components shown in Table 1 are quite highly correlated—that is, countries at the top in education tend to be at the top in plant and equipment and in efficiency. My research with Jones explored the underlying determinants of the three components. We asked the question, what fundamental factor results in the accumulation of high levels of education, large stocks of plant and equipment, and in a high level of efficiency? Our answer focuses on social infrastructure. Some

TABLE 1.   Data on Output per Worker and Its Three
            Determinants, for Selected Countries

Country	Output per worker	Contribution from		
		Education	Plant and equipment	Efficiency
United States	1.000	1.000	1.000	1.000
Canada	0.941	0.908	1.002	1.034
Italy	0.834	0.650	1.063	1.207
West Germany	0.818	0.802	1.118	0.912
France	0.818	0.666	1.091	1.126
United Kingdom	0.727	0.808	0.891	1.011
Hong Kong	0.608	0.735	0.741	1.115
Singapore	0.606	0.545	1.031	1.078
Japan	0.587	0.797	1.119	0.658
Mexico	0.433	0.538	0.868	0.926
Argentina	0.418	0.676	0.953	0.648
U.S.S.R.	0.417	0.724	1.231	0.468
India	0.086	0.454	0.709	0.267
China	0.060	0.632	0.891	0.106
Kenya	0.056	0.457	0.747	0.165
Zaire	0.033	0.408	0.499	0.160

(SOURCE: See Figure 2.)

countries have institutions that promote accumulation and efficiency. Where the social infrastructure is strong, businesses and workers concentrate on productive activities. They do not fear the loss of the fruits of their efforts to parasites. More than anything else, strong infrastructure means an effective rule of law.

Government provides most of the social infrastructure that promotes accumulation of human and physical capital and the achievement of high levels of efficiency. Government enforces laws against thievery, squatting, Mafia activities, and other crimes that divert output from those who create it.

Government enforces private contracts, a key part of the infrastructure. Government establishes effective property rights. But government may also contribute to diverting output through taxation, expropriation, and corruption. An effective government uses an efficient tax system with non-confiscatory tax rates. It avoids expropriating businesses and pays market value when it takes property from the public. Corruption is perhaps the most important threat. In countries with weak infrastructure, government officials use their positions to steal from productive people and businesses.

One of our findings is that the effectiveness of government is more important than the relative role of private and public economic activity. A government that largely suppresses corruption and other forms of government-sponsored diversion, but with a large involvement in the economy in the forms of government-operated businesses and aggressive tax-transfer programs, can still create an environment conducive to capital accumulation and productive efficiency. Sweden and France are good examples. Even the Soviet Union, where the government ran almost the whole economy, achieved levels of capital accumulation not too far behind the United States and a level of efficiency almost half that of the United States. By contrast, India and China, with much less effective governments, were one-fourth and one-tenth as efficient as the United States in 1988.

Jones and I calculated an index of social infrastructure from data on corruption, expropriation, law enforcement, and other dimensions of government effectiveness. Figure 6 displays the values of our index in the same format as earlier figures. The countries at the top, with index values at about one-third the of U.S. level, have high levels of corruption, poor enforcement of criminal and contract law, ineffective property rights, high rates of Mafia-type activities, and frequent government expropriation. The rewards for business activity in those countries are few. Capable people go into criminal and other parasitical activities rather than produce goods and services. The countries at the bottom have strictly

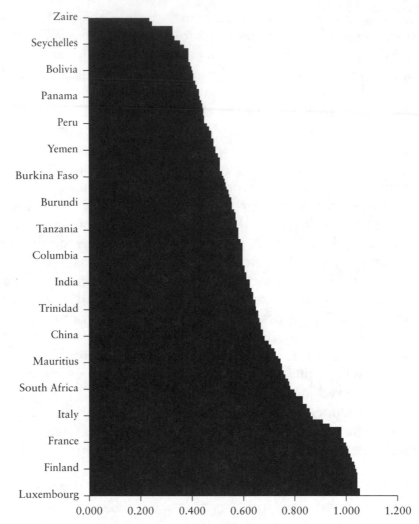

FIGURE 6. Index of Social Infrastructure, with United States at 1.0
(SOURCE: See Figure 2)

honest governments, effective courts for law enforcement with capable, honest judges, police forces that deter crime by aggressive pursuit of the small number of criminals, and governments that respect property rights and do not expropriate private economic gains. Although the United States scores high in these measures, it is not at the top. Most of the countries

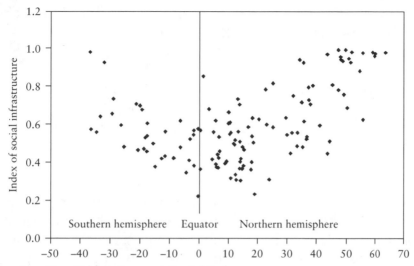

FIGURE 7.   Education and Social Infrastructure

(SOURCE: See Figure 2)

in northwest Europe score somewhat higher, as does Canada.

Countries with strong social infrastructures foster accumulation of human capital. They send large numbers of children and young adults to private and public schools, colleges, and universities. Figure 7 shows the relationship in our set of countries between our index of infrastructure and our index of education. The countries in the upper right—mostly in Western Europe, North America, and east Asia—have capable, honest governments. In most of them, government is the primary provider of education. They have high stocks of human capital. The countries in the lower left have corrupt, ineffective governments. Neither the government nor private education function well. Workers are poorly educated and output per worker is low.

What factors lead a country to adopt an effective social infrastructure? We don't have a complete answer to this question, but history sheds some light. The principles of government that yield high scores in the measures that go into our index of infrastructure originated in Western Europe in the years leading up to the late eighteenth century. The publication of Adam Smith's *Wealth of Nations* in 1776 marked the full development of the ideas, although their adoption took two more centuries. The principles spread over the globe unevenly. Colonialism was an important factor, but becoming a colony of a European power was no guarantee of later development of favorable infrastructure, as the cases of India and Bolivia demonstrate, with infrastructure indexes of about 0.6 and 0.4 respectively.

Recent thinking about the development of infrastructure emphasizes the importance of settlement in a colony.[4] Colonialism had two versions. In one—applicable to the United States, Canada, Australia, and to some extent Argentina— the colonial power conquered land thinly populated by nomads. Settlers brought institutions and infrastructure from the home country. In the United States, infrastructure soon outstripped England's, as the largely self-governing colonies developed more efficient and honest governments.

In the second version of colonialism, its dark side, the purpose of conquest was exploitation of an existing population. The home country sent administrators and soldiers, not settlers. The colonial power functioned as a diverter of value from existing economies. India is a leading example. Britain never introduced British government to India, nor did many of the British settle there. Rather, British policy was to make alliances with existing government units whose infrastructure was altogether different. The British in India governed by corrupting governments. The adverse effects of colonialism in Africa need no comment. Spanish and Portuguese colonial policies in Latin America were generally extractive rather than transplantive. Chile has succeeded in creating a reasonably favorable infrastructure, but equatorial Latin America still mainly has governments with low infrastructure scores.

The choice between the two colonial models was not by chance. Settlement occurred in the kind of temperate climates familiar to Europeans. The United States, Canada,

Australia, and New Zealand all offered healthy climates. They also lacked indigenous populations with systems of property rights recognized by the British. In their colonies, the law-abiding British respected existing systems of property rights resembling the British system, where property owners marked their land and generally lived on it. They rejected property claims of nomads.

Acemoglu and his co-authors point to the specific role of potential mortality as a prime determinant of the location of settlement. Mosquito-borne diseases—malaria and yellow fever—were the main cause of death of settlers in the tropics. Hence, settlers avoided low-latitude locations where mosquitoes lived year-round and thus could propagate disease. Settlement occurred at higher latitudes, whereas the extractive model, particularly in the cultivation of sugar, was adopted for low latitudes.

These patterns left a legacy plainly visible today. With the single very special exception of Singapore, countries near the equator have poor infrastructure, low levels of education and physical capital, and low efficiency. Figure 8 shows the countries that Jones and I studied, arrayed by location relative to the equator. There is an unmistakable U shape to the plot. Because the preponderance of the world's land area is north of the equator, most of the markers are to the right of the vertical line denoting the equator. In both hemispheres, the markers rise for latitudes away from the equator.

The marker just to the right of the equator line in Figure 8 and well above the others for equatorial countries is Singapore. This country validates the underlying ideas about infrastructure, even though it is a notable exception to the rule that tropical countries have poor infrastructure. Singapore was an uninhabited island claimed by the British in the early nineteenth century as a military base. British policy never attempted to extract value from the population that gradually developed, mostly Chinese but with a significant Malay minority. Rather, the British allowed the development of British institutions and infrastructure.

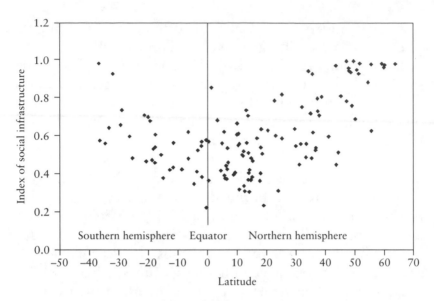

FIGURE 8.   Location and Social Infrastructure
(SOURCE: See Figure 2)

The pattern of education over the globe tracks the pattern of infrastructure. Countries in higher latitudes, more likely to have strong infrastructure, accumulate more human capital. Figure 9 shows the U-shaped relation between our education index and latitude. Singapore is not a standout in education because such a large fraction of its population comprises recent immigrants from countries such as China with poor infrastructure and correspondingly little education.

CONCLUSIONS

Global evidence shows that education contributes to national productivity as well as to individual earnings. Countries with strong institutions and infrastructure, and effective governments, arrange to provide their citizens with substantial amounts of education, sometimes exceeding the U.S. level. Accumulation of human capital is one of the three important benefits that flow from good infrastructure; the others are

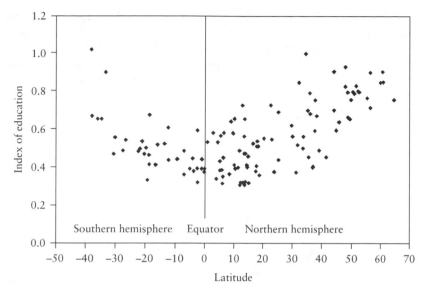

FIGURE 9. Location and Education
(SOURCE: See Figure 2)

accumulation of plant and equipment and the development of efficient production.

The countries of the world that have achieved high levels of education for the average person have done so in varying combinations of self-finance, government subsidy, and direct provision of education. One of the few favorable characteristics of the discredited socialist governments of Eastern Europe was the provision of high levels of education. As the relative cost of education continues to rise in relation to other goods and services, the strain to finance high levels of education will worsen.

NOTES

1. George Psacharopoulos, "Returns to Investment in Education: A Global Update," *World Development* 22 (1994):1325–43.
2. Robert Summers and Alan Heston, "The Penn World Table (Mark 5): An Expanded Set of International Comparison:1950–1988," *Quarterly Journal of Economics* 106(1991): 327–68. The data, updated, are available from http://pwt. econ.upenn.edu/.

3. Robert E. Hall and Charles I. Jones, "Why Do Some Countries
   Produce So Much More Output per Worker Than Others?" *Quarterly Journal of Economics* 114(February 1999): 83–116.
4. Daron Acemoglu, Simon Johnson, and James Robinson, "The
   Colonial Origins of Comparative Development: An Empirical Investigation," NBER Working Paper no. 7771, June 2000.

Redistributional Consequences of Educational Reform

Paul M. Romer

To an economist, the fundamental problem in elementary and secondary school education seems simple. Throughout the world, government funding for education has been unnecessarily equated with government operation of the schools. According to this interpretation, the solution is equally simple: maintain government funding but privatize the schools. Specifically, let a variety of private organizations operate schools, let parents choose among them, and let the government compensate the schools on the basis of the number and type of children that they attract and how well their students perform. On the face of it, this approach would continue to make education freely available to all children and still let a nation capture the gains associated with competition and free entry in the provision of educational services.

If this economic analysis captured the essence of the problem in education, it would surely be a simple matter to put together a broad political coalition that would support the privatization of government-run school systems. The efficiency gains from privatization would be large. Under this strategy, they seemingly can be achieved with no reduction in the commitment that a society makes to help the disadvantaged. There would, of course, be a small group of self-interested individuals who have an economic interest in the preservation of the existing state-run system. They would resist any change but would be overwhelmingly outnumbered by parents and other concerned citizens. Yet, despite four decades of debate, proposals for voucher-style privatization schemes have made remarkably little progress in the developed world in general, and in the United States in particular. There must be something that the economic analysis misses.

To a politician and a voter, the fundamental problem in elementary and secondary school education is more complex. The gap in the economic analysis lies in its implicit assumption that it will be possible to maintain the same level of government support for the education of children from poor families under an alternative system based on private provision of educational services. It assumes that the level of public support for education and the mechanism for delivering the educational services can be chosen independently. The politician and the voter recognize, however, that the level of public funding for education is the outcome of a political process and that changes in the delivery system can induce changes in this level of funding.

As a result, the challenge that reformers face in designing a proposal for reforming education goes beyond the one assumed in the standard economic analysis. To attract broad support, a reform proposal must simultaneously increase efficiency in the delivery of educational services and maintain the level of redistribution that emerges from the political processes determining the level of support for education.

WHY SHOULD SOCIETY REDISTRIBUTE INCOME, AND WHY USE SCHOOLS TO DO IT?

Because redistribution lies at the heart of the current impasse over school reform, it is useful to step back and review the logic behind the two premises shared by the economic and

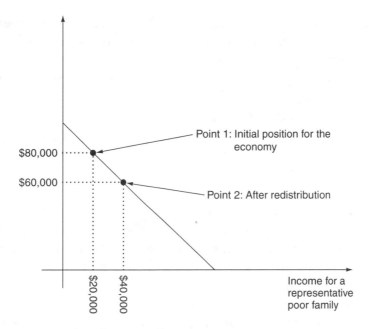

FIGURE 1. Redistribution of Income

political analyses of school reform: (1) The government should redistribute income from the rich to the poor, (2) The school system should be one of the vehicles that the government uses to implement a program of redistribution.

Figure 1 illustrates the usual framing of discussions about the redistribution of income. Point 1 illustrates income levels for representative rich and poor families. By assumption, these incomes are determined by the operation of a competitive market system.

The most fundamental result in economics tells us that, to a first approximation, the market system is efficient in the sense that it maximizes total income available to a society. This result is often referred to as the "invisible hand" theorem because of Adam Smith's famous assertion that in a competitive market, each person ". . . intends only his own gain, and he is in this, as in many other cases, led by an invisible hand to promote an end which was no part of his intention. . . . By pursuing his own interest he frequently promotes that of the society more effectually than when he really intends to promote it."

In a hypothetical society made up of equal numbers of rich and poor families, total income is signified in the Figure by the position of the downward sloping line. Along this line, the sum of the income for the rich and the poor families is constant. The points on the line represent all the possible divisions of total income between these two types of families. According to the invisible hand theorem, if a government assigns and enforces ownership rights for the productive resources in an economy and lets people trade these resources in a competitive market, market forces ensure that total income is maximized. The line will be shifted out as far to the right as possible.

In political debates, this powerful result is sometimes used to support a limited role for the government, a role that extends only to establishing and enforcing property rights. This use of the theorem fails to take account of its full implications. In the process of maximizing total income and pushing the downward sloping line out to the right, the market selects a division of income among the various market participants. That is, at the same time that it determines a position for the line, it also picks a point on the line, a point such as Point 1 in Figure 1. The invisible hand theorem is silent about the merits of this particular division of total income.

There is a clear sense in which different positions of the downward sloping line can be ranked from worse to better. More total income for society is unambiguously better than less. A market system supported by a limited government has an advantage because it maximizes total income. But in contrast to the different positions of the entire line, points on a specific line cannot be ranked. Moving along a line makes one family better-off but another worse-off, and there is no scientific way to determine whether any movement along the line is good or bad. Economics as a science has absolutely nothing to say about what would be an efficient, desirable, or appropriate distribution of income. In particular, it does not provide any basis for arguing that the particular division of income that results from market competition has any special moral, ethical, or philosophical justification.

Although economics does not give us any basis for saying that an outcome such as Point 2 in the Figure is better or worse than a less-equal outcome such as Point 1, individual people do have preferences over the distribution of income. Most people seem to prefer outcomes like Point 2, in which income is more equally distributed, to outcomes like Point 1, in which it is less equally distributed. This preference is particularly clear when a person expresses preferences over the incomes of others. Of course, people tend to prefer more income for themselves, but holding their own income constant, they prefer more equal divisions of income among others. Faced with a choice, people also seem to be willing to agree to a tradeoff between these two goals. They will sacrifice some of their income if, in so doing, they can raise standards of living for the most disadvantaged. We see evidence of this willingness both in political support for redistribution and in individual decisions about charitable giving.

There is nothing paradoxical about the claim that economics as a science has nothing to say about what constitutes an appropriate division of income but that people do have preferences over the division of income. This is analogous to the claim that economics does not have anything to say about whether people prefer drinking wine or salt water with their meals, but that people do have meaningful preferences about which is better. Economic theory does not prescribe what tastes people should have. It observes that the best way to achieve high levels of satisfaction is to give people the opportunity to make their own choices. In the same way, economics does not prescribe any particular division of income but suggests that people in a society may be better-off if they are free to make a decision about what that division should be.

The difficulty associated with a change in the distribution of income is that it is a choice that must be made collectively.

Both you and I care about the distribution of income between two other families. If this distribution is changed somehow, it affects both of us. As a result, societies must use a nonmarket mechanism for aggregating all the different preferences that people like you and me have over the distribution of income and selecting a distribution of income that will prevail.

The typical way in which this collective decision-making process operates is for people to vote. For example, they can decide by majority rule whether to adopt a system of taxes paid by the rich and transfers given to the poor. As before, imagine that Figure 1 represents income levels in a society with equal numbers of rich and poor families. If they were faced with a yes-or-no decision, a majority of citizens might vote in favor of a system that takes $20,000 from each rich family and gives a transfer of $20,000 to each poor family. If so, this society can move from the unequal distribution of income represented by Point 1 toward the more equal distribution represented by Point 2. Some people may have preferred more redistribution. Others may have preferred less. But many people, perhaps even everyone, may prefer a world described by Point 2 instead of one described by Point 1.

The simple argument in favor of minimal government advocates the use of the market on grounds of efficiency. A more nuanced economic argument in favor of the market outlines a two-step procedure that expands the role of the government. First, the government should maximize total income by adopting a market system. Second, it should use a system of taxes and transfers to achieve a distribution of income that is preferred by a large fraction of the votes to the distribution selected by the market. Without this second step, the members of a society would not, in general, be able to achieve a distribution of income that they prefer to the one determined by the market.

A government can be essential for achieving this outcome. If there were no collective element to the decision-making process, people could adjust the distribution of income by unilateral action—for example, by giving to charity. People do give to charity, but because of what economists call the "free-rider problem," unilateral chari-table giving is unlikely to achieve the distribution of in-come that most people would prefer. This is true even if there is unanimity between all members of society over the outcome that would be preferred. Suppose, for example, that everyone—even the rich families that would have to give up $20,000 of their income —would prefer Point 2 in Figure 1 to Point 1. That is, each rich family is willing to give up $20,000 to be able to increase the income of each poor family from $20,000 to $40,000. But suppose that there are 1,000 rich families and 1,000 poor families. Sup-pose that the other 999 rich families have all given $20,000 to charities that redistribute the income to poor families, so that poor families have income after transfers equal to $20,000 + [(999/1000) \times $20,000] = $39,980. Suppose you are making decisions for the remaining rich family. If you give up $20,000 in income, you can raise the income of each poor family from $39,980 to $40,000. Although you were willing to give up $20,000 to raise the income of every poor family from $20,000 to $40,000, you might not be willing to give up $20,000 to raise the income of each poor family from $39,980 to $40,000. Because all the other rich families are giving a portion of their income to raise the income of the poor, you may be tempted to shirk, or "free ride" on, their contributions and not to make any of your own. But, of course, the same possibility will occur to other rich families. If each rich family is free to choose whether to contribute, many of them may choose not to contribute and to leave the problem to others. In the end, this could lead to the absence of effective redistribution, an outcome that none of the rich families desired.

The key to giving a society the ability to achieve a point like Point 2 that everyone prefers is to give the rich families some way to write a binding contract among themselves, one that can avoid the free-rider problem. The essence of this contract is that, once the desired level of redistribution has been set, everyone is obligated to contribute. In effect, each rich family is obliged to make its contribution with the knowledge that all other rich families are similarly bound. This is precisely what a mandatory tax-and-transfer system can achieve. No voluntary system of charitable donations can replicate this kind of binding agreement.

The outline of a two-step model of economic organization—establish a market system and establish a tax and transfer system to achieve the desired level of redistribution—leaves unresolved a number of ambiguities about how a society reaches a decision concerning the amount of redistribution to undertake. It also says nothing about how it is that members of a society come to have preferences over abstractions such as the distribution of income and about the definition of the group within which the distribution of income is measured. These ambiguities are central to the debate about school reform, and they will resurface shortly. But before turning to them, I will explore two further points about the connection between efficiency and the distribution of income.

THE STATIC TRADEOFF BETWEEN EFFICIENCY AND EQUITY

Figure 2 gives an expanded look at the possible effects of a system designed to redistribute income. In Figure 2, the shift from Point 1 to Point 2 implicitly assumed that redistribution could take place without any loss of efficiency. In terms of the description in that Figure, this meant that it was possible to move along the line that holds total income constant. In general, this kind of movement may not be possible. Many forms of redistribution entail a loss of efficiency.

To give a simple illustration of these efficiency losses, a tax that causes a reduction in income of $20,000 for a rich family may generate only $10,000 in revenue for the government. The rich family may give up a net of $10,000 in resources, complying with the tax laws or implementing tax avoidance strategies, and then pay an additional $10,000 to the government. If the $10,000 in actual revenue that the government collects is given to the poor family as a cash transfer, the family's income goes up by the full $10,000. Yet the income of the rich family (after paying its taxes and its compliance and avoidance costs) goes down by the full $20,000. This causes a loss of efficiency, a reduction in total income for society as a whole. In Figure 2, this is represented by Point 3, which lies below the line passing through Point 1. In the jargon of economics, we say that the taxes impose "distortions," "deadweight losses," or "efficiency costs."

A less obvious point, but one that may be at least as important for policy purposes, comes not on the tax collection side but on the transfer side. Suppose that by offering the $10,000 transfer to the poor family, the government inadvertently encourages members of the family to undertake actions that also reduce total income in society. For example, suppose that the government pays this transfer to anyone who drops out of high school and gives birth to a child. It is possible that, in so doing, the government could dissuade some people from continuing their schooling, people who could have completed more schooling and gone on to become members of rich families. Because these people do not acquire as much education as they would have but for the transfer, they earn less. Total income for society is reduced. Hence, there can be efficiency costs associated with both the collection of the tax revenue and the transfer of income. Both the tax and the transfer can change behavior in ways that reduce total income.

Private charitable giving has drawn increased political support because of a growing perception that some government spending programs, such as cash transfers for unwed mothers, may impose higher costs for society than comparable levels of spending by private charitable organizations. When people advocate a shift away from government programs and toward charitable mechanisms for redistributing income, they make the same mistake as the

defenders of the existing public school system. They equate
the financing mechanism with the delivery system. Just as it
is possible to use government funding to pay private providers of educational services, it is possible to use government funding to pay private providers of social services. It
is not necessary that we shift to a voluntary system of funding to get the benefits of private provision of services. This
is important because voluntary systems of funding will always suffer from the free-rider problem described in the
previous section.

Point 4 in Figure 2 illustrates the effect of an opposing
force that could in principle be strong enough to offset the
efficiency losses associated with spending on redistribution. If this effect is large enough, it can overturn the usual
tradeoff between efficiency and equity. Point 4 suggests
there are some forms of redistribution that can increase efficiency. Suppose once again that the government collects
$10,000 in income from the rich family and does so at a
cost of $20,000 in lost consumption opportunities for the
rich family. The process of collecting the taxes still causes
$10,000 in efficiency losses.

But suppose that the government spends the $10,000 in
revenue on additional education for a worker from the poor
family, and that this extra education increases the market
wage of this worker by $30,000. In this case, total income for
the society can go up, even after taking account of the distortions imposed on the rich family by the tax. As suggested
by Point 4, total income for the two families can increase to
$110,000, up from $100,000. The $10,000 efficiency cost of
the tax on the rich family is more than offset by the $20,000
net efficiency gain associated with the increased investment in
education for the member of the poor family.

The numbers here are not intended to be realistic, and
they skip over the issue of how to compare a one-time expenditure on education with a lifetime of higher earnings. If
you think about the analogy with investment in financial assets, you can see that the right way to do this would be to

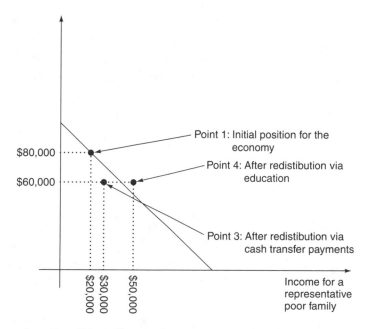

FIGURE 2.   Possible Effects of System to Redistribute Income

calculate a rate of return on the investment in education. All that matters for the discussion here is that the rate of return on investments in education may be very high, so high that society as a whole is better off if the government increases its support for education.

This kind of outcome, one in which the government raises total income for society by subsidizing education, can arise only if the invisible hand theorem fails. Recall that this theorem says that the market will maximize total income all by itself, with no intervention by the government. The logic of the theorem, applied to this situation, is as follows. If it is possible for a poor worker to earn benefits from education that exceed the costs of acquiring the education, then self-interested poor workers should arrange to receive the extra education. If the market worked perfectly, the poor worker would be able to borrow money, spend it on education, use the higher wages that result to pay off the loan, and still have extra income left over to improve the quality of life.

There are two well-known reasons why the market mechanism might not lead to sufficient investment in education and might thereby cause the invisible hand theorem to fail. The first problem is that a poor worker might not be able to borrow to finance education for herself (or her children). Lenders might not be able to collect on loans made to finance education because there is nothing that they can repossess if the borrower defaults. As a result, they are unwilling to lend. It is because of this first problem that the government offers guaranteed student loans to children from poor families who want to attend college.

A second and more difficult problem, one that is much more important for an analysis of elementary and secondary schooling, is that the educational investments need to be made on behalf of a child. School-age children may not be either legally or intellectually competent to make an informed decision about the costs and benefits of an investment that will pay returns for decades into the future. Unfortunately, some parents may not be willing or able to make the investments on their children's behalf that are required to achieve full efficiency. In effect, the parents may be in the same position as the bank. It would be efficient for them to finance an investment in education for their children and then to have their children repay them later in life. But like the bank, the parents may be incapable of collecting on investments such as these that pay off much later in life.[1] For this reason, governments have not only financed educational expenses but have also made attendance at primary and secondary schools mandatory. Governments require by law that parents send their children to school.

THE DYNAMIC TRADEOFF BETWEEN EFFICIENCY AND EQUITY

Section 1 presented the justification for the first of the two premises from which all discussions of educational reform proceed. Governments redistribute income because voters care about inequality. Section 2 addresses the second premise. Governments use subsidies for education as a mechanism for undertaking the redistribution because it is a form of transfer to poor families that is likely to be less harmful to efficiency than other transfer mechanisms, such as cash transfers. Subsidies for education may even improve efficiency.

Each of the justifications for these premises is based on a static analysis, one assuming that the underlying structure of the economy does not change. The next step is to think about how changes in the economy affect the analysis. As it turns out, changes in our economy reinforce both presumptions: that the government should redistribute income and that support for education is an efficient way to achieve more equal economic outcomes in a society.

Figure 3 illustrates the situation that now confronts the developed countries of the world. Points 1 and 5 illustrate the positions of the economy before and after a change in its structure. In moving from Point 1 to Point 5, the sum of income for the two representative families goes up from $100,000 to $140,000, but the distribution becomes more unequal. It shifts from a split of $80,000 and $20,000 to a split of $130,000 and $10,000.

This kind of change in the structure of an economy presents society with a more important tradeoff between efficiency and inequality than the one that is assumed in the static analysis from Figure 2. Citizens in the world illustrated in Figure 3 can increase both efficiency and inequality by letting this change in the structure take place, or they can reduce efficiency and inequality by blocking the change. If these are the only choices that are available to an economy, the tradeoff between efficiency and redistribution is stark. Out of a natural concern for their own well-being and that of their children, parents from a poor family will naturally try to block this kind of change. So might rich, altruistic families.

One would hope that economic progress did not present society with this kind of dilemma, but unfortunately two of

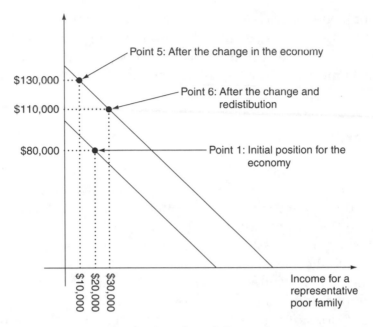

FIGURE 3.   Situation in the Developed Countries

the most important driving forces in the modern economy
have precisely this character. Both technological change and
increased trade between developed and developing nations
are likely to increase inequality at the same time that they increase efficiency.

Evidence from labor markets suggests that technological
change increases the demand for highly educated workers
and reduces the demand for less educated workers and has
done so since the early years of the twentieth century.[2] To
appreciate how this kind of process can arise, picture the effects of technological change in telephony. When telephone
systems were first installed, the phone company employed an
operator, with little schooling or technical training, who put
plugs into a switchboard to connect calls. Then engineers
working for the phone system developed electromechanical
switches that could connect lines in response to the electrical

pulses sent by the dialing phone. This technological advance raised efficiency and reduced the cost of phone service, but it reduced the demand for relatively less-skilled operators who formerly made the connections. It also increased the demand for the higher-skilled workers who could design and maintain the electromechanical switches.

More recently, computer switches have replaced these electromechanical switches. New technologies such as voice recognition are further reducing demand for the less-skilled workers who currently provide services such as directory assistance. These technologies are raising the demand for highly skilled workers who can install and maintain these complicated computer switches.

These changes in the technology for providing phone service are representative of changes that have taken place throughout the economy. In manufacturing, and especially in agriculture, technological change has steadily reduced the number of less-skilled workers needed to produce a given amount of output.

If the relative supply of different types of workers had stayed constant over the course of the twentieth century, the demand shifts caused by technological change would have steadily increased the wages of the more-educated workers and reduced the wages of the less-educated workers. In this sense, technological change seems to present society with the dilemma illustrated in Figure 3—but only *seems*, because there is a way out. Fortunately, the relative supplies did not stay constant. The various levels of government in the United States made massive investments in elementary, secondary, and tertiary education and dramatically reduced the fraction of the labor force with low levels of education. As a result of these investments, the economy in the United States moved not to a position such as Point 5, but instead to a new position such as Point 6 in Figure 3. By itself, technological change would have moved the economy toward a position such as Point 5, but the combination of technological change and large government-financed investments in education moved the economy to a position such as Point 6.

Of course, one can argue that in principle, people could have made the same kind of investment in education even if the government had not financed it. This is the parallel to the argument noted above that poor people should always be able to borrow and finance the efficient level of education. However, the historical correlation of high levels of school enrollment with high levels of government support for schooling suggests that government funding does lead to substantially higher levels of educational attainment, and hence to less income inequality than would prevail without government support.[3]

The available evidence points to a continuation of the trend from the twentieth century. Technological change will continue to raise productivity and increase total income. But acting alone, it will tend to do so in ways that lead to concentrated income gains for the best-educated families and quite possibly to losses for families with the lowest levels of education. This sets up what Katz and Goldin (1996) called *a race between technological change and government investment in education*. If the government can keep increasing the average level of educational achievement in a society rapidly enough to keep up with technological change, it can ensure that economic growth leads to gains for all segments of the population. Even the workers who remain less educated will face rising wages over time because the investment in education means that there will be fewer less-educated workers such as themselves competing for the jobs that they can do. In effect, the government can raise wages for workers with less education by creating a shortage of these workers.

If the government falls behind in this race, income inequality will widen. During the 1970s and 1980s, government investment in education did not seem to keep up.[4] Wages for workers with low levels of education remained constant or fell at the same time that wages for workers with high levels of education continued to grow.

The challenge posed by a process of technological change that increases the demand for highly educated workers is larger than many people realize. It will not be enough to return our school system back to the level of achievement of an average or even good school at some point in the past. During this century the United States will need to increase overall educational attainment dramatically just to keep up with the ongoing process of technological change. If it fails to do so, a growing segment of the population will suffer a reduction in their economic opportunities. As a result, many people will naturally support proposals designed to slow progress and limit trade.

The other change in the economy that will have the same kind of effect as technological change will be increased trade between the rich and poor nations of the world. Technological change will continue to reduce transportation and communication costs. Poor countries will increasingly recognize that it is in their interest to trade with the rich countries of the world. Because the poor countries have relatively abundant supplies of less-skilled labor, supplies that are very large compared to the size of the workforce in the developed world, the effects of this increased trade will be to put additional downward pressure on wages for less-skilled workers in the developed countries.

The effects on the distribution of income will be even larger if workers with low levels of skill are free to migrate to countries such as the United States. In effect, the education-based strategy followed in the United States for more than a century has been to create a shortage of workers with low levels of skill. This raises the wage for a less-skilled worker in the United States relative to what it would otherwise have been. As long as there is a large pool of less-skilled workers in the rest of the world, free international migration of workers can completely undercut a strategy of driving up wages for less-skilled workers by making this type of worker relatively scarce.

In all likelihood, international migration will be tightly regulated in years to come. But one would hope that the processes of trade and globalization could proceed. The efficiency gains that remain to be exploited are too large to forgo. If these gains are not realized, firms in the United States will increasingly find that they can shift production activities that require only high school–educated workers to parts of the world where high school–educated workers earn far less than they do here. If these firms do not do so, they will find that they are driven out of business by new firms that spring up in these areas.

If, by the end of this century, most workers in the United States have high levels of education, this process need not lead to increased wage inequality within its borders. Assuming that barriers to immigration persist, the relatively few workers in the United States who have low levels of skill will be well compensated for doing the less-skilled jobs that are difficult to move abroad. But if the United States falls behind in the race to raise education levels and continues to have large numbers of workers with only a high school education, these workers could see their wages fall toward the level that prevails in the rest of the world as trade expands.

These changes—technological progress and increased international trade—mean that countries such as the United States will face a very different kind of tradeoff between efficiency and income inequality than the static tradeoff illustrated in Figure 1. If large numbers of citizens find that these twin forces are reducing their income and that no offsetting policy response moderates these effects, they will use the political system to slow down these forces. Even affluent families may support measures designed to limit technological change and trade if they think that this is the only way to preserve existing levels of income for poor families. Resistance to free trade, which simmers just below the surface in domestic political debate, could quickly become a powerful political force. Legislation designed to protect the income of less-skilled workers could easily act as a brake on the adoption of new technology.

In Figure 3, if a poor family is offered a choice between Points 1 and 5, they will surely opt for Point 1, even though it means that the economy fails to take advantage of large potential efficiency gains. A society may be able to maintain a political consensus in favor of both technological progress and free trade only if it can find ways to transfer some of the gains that these forces can generate to workers from poor families.

THE REQUIRED INVESTMENT IN EDUCATION

U.S. citizens can continue using education as a way to create a relatively homogeneous society, one that does not suffer from the extremes of income inequality that we see in other countries of the world. If this happens, it should be possible to maintain a political consensus in favor of continued technological change and increased international trade. But this path will not be easy. The education race is going to become more challenging in the coming century, and there are clear indications that our educational institutions are not performing well.

To show just how hard this challenge is, suppose that the near future resembles the recent past. In 1940, only 25 percent of the population in the United States had completed high school. Sixty years later, in 2000, a high school degree is considered the minimum acceptable level of education for a new entrant in the job market. Over 80 percent of the adults in the United States now have a high school degree.

In 2000, the degree held by the top 25 percent of the population was a tertiary degree—either a bachelor's degree from a college or university or an associate degree from a junior college or vocational school. If past trends continue,

in sixty years a tertiary degree or its equivalent may become
the new minimum standard for entry into the job market. By
then we may need to aim for universal completion of a tertiary degree just as we now aim for universal completion of
high school. Our primary and secondary schools will therefore have to prepare virtually all students for advanced
study. To do this for students from the bottom half of the
achievement distribution, our school system will have to do
a much better job.

The available indicators suggest that the United States at
present does a particularly bad job of educating students
from the least-advantaged backgrounds. The Organization
for Economic Cooperation and Development (OECD) has
used a standardized set of materials to test the prose, document, and quantitative literacy skills of a representative
sample of adults in most of its member countries. The average score in the United States is comparable to that in most
other countries but there are many more people here who
have very low levels of basic literacy skills, more than other
nations at a comparable level of development. For example,
reading abilities at the 5th percentile in the distribution are
markedly lower in the United States than in any country in
Western Europe (Figure 2.1).[5]

When the data are analyzed by cohort, it also becomes
clear that most other countries have been able to increase
mean literacy scores from one generation to the next. For
example, people in Canada who are between the ages of 46
and 65 and who were graduated from high school between
thirty and fifty years ago perform, on average, at about the
same level on all three measures of literacy as people in the
United States who were graduated from high school at the
same time. Over time, schools there seem to have been
doing a better job. People in Canada who were graduated
from high school more recently score at higher levels than
the people from older cohorts.

In the United States, there is no such evidence of im
provement. People who have graduated from high school

more recently do not do any better on the literacy tests than the 46–65-year-olds who graduated from high school thirty to sixty years ago. In this regard, it is the United States, not Canada, that is unusual. Other countries such as Poland and Hungary, which have lower levels of literacy for older cohorts than the United States, and countries such as the Netherlands and Sweden, which have higher levels of literacy for older cohorts than the United States, show big improvements in the abilities of the people who were graduated from high school more recently.

ALTERNATIVE MECHANISMS FOR REDISTRIBUTING INCOME

It will be hard to keep up in the education race as this century advances. It will also be hard to implement true educational reform in the context of an education system that is intended to reduce inherited inequality. If there were a viable alternative that would preserve something like the current distribution of income, one that would make sure that all families share in the coming gains from technological change and increased trade, it would make sense to adopt it. If we could relieve education of the burden of being our primary program for reducing inequality, it would be much easier to reform the educational system and raise the level of its performance. Unfortunately, there are no good alternatives for redistributing income.

As the discussion in Section 2 has already suggested, direct cash transfers have proven to be an unworkable way to deal with growing income inequality because of the changes in behavior and the high efficiency costs they induce. The policy experiment with more generous cash support levels that was undertaken in the United States and Europe in the last three decades has convinced voters and policymakers that these transfers reduce employment, encourage antisocial behavior, and create an intergenerational cycle of dependency that is costly for society as a whole. The only exception to this general rule may be the case of cash transfers to the elderly, which are not perceived to have high social costs.

Governments could replace unconditional cash transfers to young workers with subsidies for low-wage employment. In the United States, the imposition of time limits on eligibility for welfare payments, together with a more generous Earned Income Tax Credit, has had the effect of shifting our tax and transfer system in this direction.

In contrast to government support for education, which takes decades to have its full effect, a wage subsidy for low-income workers has the advantage that it can raise take-home pay quickly. But over a longer time horizon, the relative merit of the two strategies shifts. Over time, wage subsidies will have trouble keeping up with the cumulative effect of the forces that will impinge on the economy.

Suppose that, during the next century, technological change and increased trade will lead to an average rate of growth of real gross domestic product per capita of about 1.5 percent per year. This means that after correcting for inflation, total income from all sources, divided by the population, will increase by about 1.5 percent per year. To keep the argument here conservative, this rate is less than the 1.8 percent real rate of growth sustained in the twentieth century. Because wages tend to be a constant fraction of GDP or total output for a society, this means that, on average, total wages will also increase by 1.5 percent per year. Suppose that in the absence of any policy that offsets the effects of technological change and trade, this average increase would take the form of no wage growth for high school–educated workers and rapid wage growth for highly educated workers. (In the 1970s and 1980s, wages for high school–educated workers actually fell, so this is not an unreasonable assumption.) Through the power of compound interest, GDP per capita would double in fewer than fifty years. This means that, by 2050, the wage subsidy for high school–educated workers would have to be more than 100 percent to be able to give the high school–educated workers the same doubling of after-tax income that the more highly educated workers would enjoy. This would mean that the marginal tax rate faced by all workers would have to be very high just to finance the transfers required to keep the relative distribution of wages constant.

The problem that arises here is common to all wage subsidy or negative income tax proposals. To have a large effect on the distribution of income, they have to rely on very high marginal tax rates. Because the distortions associated with income taxes grow very rapidly as the marginal tax rate increases, this type of tax and transfer system would impose extremely large efficiency losses. It is highly unlikely that it would prove to be politically acceptable. Moreover, with the passage of time, the efficiency costs would grow and political support would fall as the required marginal tax rate grew.

In the long run, the steadily increasing marginal tax rates make a wage subsidy a very inefficient way to deal with pressures on the distribution of income that will arise from increased trade and more technological change. The flip side of this observation is that a subsidy for education becomes even more efficient as time passes. The rates of return to education are already very high and the level of educational attainment very low for children from disadvantaged backgrounds. The returns to more education for them seem to be far higher than the cost of the investment in the education. Hence, even now, government attempts at redistributing income that take the form of increased support for education could raise efficiency rather than lower it. And with the passage of time, the same forces that are increasing income inequality—trade and technology—will further raise the return to investments in education. Education becomes an even more efficient mechanism for raising income for people in the bottom half of the distribution of income.

As a result, on purely economic grounds the most sensible policy going forward is one that continues our current policy of using the educational system to give children from disadvantaged backgrounds better economic opportunities. The immediate challenge this poses is to find a way to reform the educational system and raise its efficiency without undermining the commitment to helping the disadvantaged. The proposal outlined in the beginning—maintaining government funding for education but privatizing the provision of educational services—seems at first to be the appropriate response to this challenge. Why, then, have voters been so hesitant to adopt this kind of reform?

MEDICARE AND MEDICAID

To understand the risks that some thoughtful people perceive from the adoption of a privatized system for delivering educational services, it helps to invoke an analogy with health care. Medicare, the health-care financing system that applies to the elderly, resembles the current public school system. Everyone over age 65 is eligible to participate and virtually everyone does. In contrast, people under the age of 65 are covered by a split or "two-tiered" system consisting of private medical insurance for the fortunate and the means-tested Medicaid program for the poor. The shift from the existing public school system to a voucher-based system could imply a shift from something like the universal Medicare program that we use for the elderly to something like the private insurance–Medicaid hybrid that we use for everyone else. Judging from the experience with these two programs, this shift would imply a substantial reduction in the commitment to helping the disadvantaged.

Medicare and Medicaid both cover the costs of medical care for the poor. The striking thing about the two programs is that Medicaid does so at levels of funding that are much lower than those offered by the Medicare program. In 1998 in the United States as a whole, the average reimbursement for a service provided under the Medicaid program was equal to 64 percent of the reimbursement for exactly the same service offered by the Medicare program.[6] Over time, this gap has been widening. Because funding decisions for Medicaid are made by the states, reimbursement rates also vary from state to state. In some states with large populations of patients on Medicaid, such as New York and California, reimbursement for a specific service such as an appendectomy under the universal Medicaid program for the elderly is less than half the reimbursement under the Medicare targeted at the poor.

The question this raises is why voters would select a health-care financing system that offers dramatically lower reimbursement rates to a poor person who is less than 65 years old than it offers for the same person when she is more than 65 years old. From the point of view of redistribution, the gap is perverse. The Medicaid program is means-tested and offered only to the most disadvantaged members of society, people who typically have more serious health problems than the rest of the population. Medicare is offered to everyone above the age of 65. A preference for redistribution toward the poor would argue for higher government reimbursement levels for services targeted at the poor, not lower levels.

When people in the Roosevelt administration began work on a comprehensive social welfare system for the United States, they had a slogan that guided their efforts: "A program for the poor is a poor program."[7] The first program that they implemented was the Social Security system for funding old-age pensions, but they anticipated that the full range of government programs would eventually grow by stages to include coverage of health-care costs, first for the elderly and then ultimately for the entire population. They and their successors were successful in creating universal service programs for Social Security and Medicare but were not able to institute a health program that covered the entire population. They settled for a health program "for the poor." They believed that despite the disadvantage of higher cost, universal service programs would provide more redistribution than programs that targeted a narrow group of poor or disadvantaged citizens. The experience with the Medicare and Medicaid programs suggests that their intuition about the politics of redistribution was correct.

A simple model that would seem at first to rationalize this observation is one based on the idea that under a program with universal coverage, rich and poor families have to consume the same level of service. Rich families will then have an incentive to lobby for a higher level of service than they would if they did not receive the service themselves. Because the service levels for all families are the same, the rich families are thereby forced to undertake more distribution than they would have selected if they could have unbundled the choice of their own service level from the level that they would provide to the poor.

This forced-redistribution model explains why it is that a universal service plan leads to more redistribution, but it does not explain why the underlying forced-redistribution plan is politically popular. If such a program were in place, it would force more redistribution than voters would otherwise select. But if voters are also given the option of shutting down the forced-redistribution plan and substituting a plan that lets them unbundle their own choices from the options that they offer to the poor, they should eagerly vote to do so. They would get rid of the universal service plan and replace it with a two-tiered, or multi-tiered, plan that has less redistribution.

This leaves a paradox. If the forced-redistribution model does not apply, this must mean that a majority of voters approve of the level of redistribution that is built into a universal service program such as Medicare. But if this is true, why would their altruism diminish when they consider the well-being of the young poor served by the Medicaid program? A preference by voters for universal service programs seems particularly hard to understand when we consider the fact that universal service programs are inherently inefficient ways to help the disadvantaged. A targeted program can avoid the efficiency cost of having a program that takes taxes away from rich families and then turns around and gives them services that they could have purchased on their own. Because there is no net redistribution to the rich, it would be more efficient for them to buy their services directly.

If a broad majority of people support the Medicare program because of the high level of redistribution that it provides, why is it not possible to transfer this political support to a targeted program for the poor? Could it provide the same level of redistribution at lower efficiency costs? For example, in the context of health care, why is it that people vote to sustain the Medicare program with its high level of redistribution but are not willing to fund the Medicaid program at comparable levels?

If voters have a "self-control problem," this behavior could be rationalized. Voters could argue that they want to provide a higher level of redistribution. They could also recognize that, if they were to make decisions about redistribution in the future in the context of choices over funding levels for a program that targets the poor, they will not support the level of redistribution that they want to select now. They could recognize that when they vote in the future about funding levels for a program that provides service to themselves, they will support higher levels of services, hence higher levels of redistribution. So as a means of tying their own hands, the voters create or maintain the universal service program.

At first, this kind of inconsistency in a voter's behavior seems hard to accept. If a thoughtful voter is in favor of redistribution now, why won't she be in favor of redistribution in the future? But this kind of inconsistency becomes easier to understand if the degree to which all voters support redistribution is a function of the amount and quality of the information that they take in about the circumstances of recipients of government aid. Suppose that someone is personally acquainted with a child who is suffering from malnutrition and sees this child face-to-face on a regular basis. This person will be very likely to give direct assistance to the child and to vote in favor of government programs that will help this child and other children who are in similar circumstances. But if, in contrast, the same observer knows in the abstract that there are children in other countries of the world who are suffering to a similar degree, the observer will typically not be willing to give as much aid to feed one of these "faceless" children.

The emotional immediacy that comes from direct face-to-face contact with people who are suffering has a very different impact on human behavior than abstract knowledge about the existence of suffering. This differential sensitivity is probably an inherent and unavoidable feature of human psychology, one that leads to striking differences in how different people see the world. To an aid worker who is distributing food to malnourished children in a country suffering from famine, it may seem monstrous that families living in the rich countries of the world spend more on food for their pets than they contribute to food for starving children. It may seem even more monstrous that these families are not even willing to support government foreign aid programs that would collect less tax from them than the amount they spend on pet food. If you consider the circumstances of the hypothetical child and the pet from the same emotional distance, it seems wrong for such a family to put the welfare of the pet ahead of the welfare of the child. But if you imagine yourself in the circumstances of the rich family, it is easy to see how normal people can behave as they do.

Any moderately educated person knows at some abstract level that there are children throughout the world who suffer terribly from deprivation that could easily be alleviated with small amounts of expenditure. We are not surprised by the fact that these people continue to lead ordinary lives, acting as if they did not know this fact, taking no step to reduce the suffering. However, because we understand the strong emotional effect that more immediate contact has on feelings of altruism toward others, we would expect that this person would respond very differently if a starving child lived next door or attended the same classes at school as their children do.

According to this kind of model, more direct personal experience with the circumstances of others leads to a stronger empathetic response to their situation. Under this model, most voters are willing to support a more generous Medicare payment system for the elderly because they have more direct personal experience with this program. Many voters in the United States have either experienced the Medicare system or know someone who has—a parent or a relative. Far fewer have the same kind of first- or second-hand experience with the grimmer Medicaid program. In the same sense that they know that there are children in parts of the world who will die from malnutrition, voters may know that there are people in the United States who receive very low levels of medical care under the Medicaid program. But in each case, this abstract knowledge has the same, greatly attenuated effect on their emotions and therefore on how they vote.

A representative voter with these kinds of experiences might therefore vote to increase spending on Medicare patients but not on Medicaid patients. She might also vote to preserve the universal coverage of the Medicare system. She realizes that were it to be converted to a means-tested program such as Medicaid, future voters like her would not provide as much support for the program, and the people that she knows and cares about would suffer.

This model does not presume any form of irrationality on the part of the voter. She may understand full well that, if she were to spend time with starving children in a foreign country, she would also vote to raise foreign aid to help these children. But in her current position, one that lets her maintain a large emotional distance from the foreign children, she has no reason to change how much of their world she experiences and how she votes on their behalf. In the same way, she has little direct experience with the welfare of poor people who use the Medicaid program and has no reason to vote to increase support for this program.

In contrast, she has detailed knowledge of the Medicare system through the experiences of the people she knows who have used this system. Because she knows what it is like for her affluent aunt to pay for her own prescription drugs, she can empathize with the burden that payments for prescription drugs impose on people like her aunt who are covered by the Medicare system. Hence she will vote to maintain the Medicare system and may even vote to expand it to cover prescription drugs, even as she votes to constrain costs in the much-less-generous Medicaid program.

Under this model, the amount of empathy any voter feels for someone else depends on how much the voter knows about the circumstances of that other person and how the voter came to know it. The more detailed and immediate information the voter has, the more readily she can imagine and feel what it would be like for the other person. When she feels more empathy, the voter will be more likely to support redistribution programs that help a disadvantaged person whose circumstances she understands.

VOTING OVER VOUCHERS

At present, many voters have direct exposure to the problems of the public school system because their children, or the children of people they know, attend these schools. In this sense, public education resembles Medicare. It is nearly a universal service program. Currently, 89 percent of primary and secondary school students in the United States attend public schools. As a result, voters as a group have more direct information about the public school system and care about the well-being of children in this system.

Voters who care about the inadequacies of the existing school system might reasonably fear that a move toward a privatized system for providing education will cause the representative voter to have less information about the educational circumstances of poor children. Most voters now have very little feel for what it is like for a poor child to be cared for under the Medicaid program. Their children and the children of most people they know are part of a very different program.

In the same way, a voucher-based system could lead to a larger separation between the educational experiences of the poor and the experiences of most other children. Under most proposals, affluent parents would be free to make additional payments for the schooling that their children receive from a private provider. As a result, affluent families will naturally tend to supplement any voucher payment and spend more on the education of their children than poor families. Schools will naturally cater to different income groups and offer higher levels of educational service to children from richer families. Over time, as these families lose direct contact with the school experience of the poor, the low quality of schools that are available to poor children in the United States will become an increasingly abstract problem, one like the problem of starving children in some foreign country. "Yes, it's a shame, but what can anyone do?"

These kinds of concerns are reinforced by the details of the specific voucher initiatives that have been offered to voters. These proposals typically offer a voucher payment that is substantially below what the government now spends on the average public school student. Judging from this evidence, it seems reasonable to project an evolution toward a system that offers very low levels of funding for the education of the poor and that offers higher quality education for the children of families that can afford to pay more.

As the nation evolves down this path, it could easily reach an equilibrium where the majority of middle- and upper-income families send their children to a private school that they pay for with a combination of a voucher worth as little as $2,000 or $3,000 per child and with a significant tuition payment of their own. As they lose contact with the rest of the school system, they will have no reason to support increases in funding for the public school system or increases in the size of the vouchers. Over time, children from very poor families will eventually face an unattractive choice between attending a private school that has to pay for its facilities and teachers on the basis of the meager voucher payments alone; or attending a public school system that suffers from a similarly low level of funding, potentially a much lower level of funding per student than the one that prevails now.

It is entirely possible that at any given level of funding, private schools for poor children will do a better job of educating poor children than the existing public school system. It is also possible that increased competition from private schools will encourage the public schools to do a better job of educating children. But at some point, reductions in funding will start to undercut the efficiencies that can be achieved through reform. As funding levels fall, the quality of schooling must ultimately fall with them.

CONCLUSION

For thoughtful voters, it would be a gamble to initiate a process that leads to a privatized provision of educational services. Many would agree that holding expenditure constant, privatization and competition would lead to significant gains in the productivity of our schools. The offsetting risk is that funding levels for the education of the poorest children might erode significantly. The gamble is whether the productivity gains will be big enough to offset the likely reductions in spending on the education of the poor. There is no question that under the existing system, children from poor families do not receive a good education in this country. However, it is possible that their educational opportunities could become even worse under a move to privatized provision of educational services. The negative effects of spending cuts could dominate the positive effects of competition and choice.

It is quite likely that children from middle- and upper-income families would benefit from a switch to the privatized system. They would get the advantages of reform, and their families could offset the reduction in funding by making their own payments for the education of their children. Parents from these families would see the beneficial effects of the change in the experiences of their children and of children that they know. They would have little direct information about the educational circumstances of the poor. As a result, the switch could lead to a new, politically stable equilibrium in which our system provides less redistribution through our educational system. It could be this prospect that makes many voters hesitate about making a fundamental change in our educational system.

Some thoughtful proponents of a privatized school system have at least begun to think about how to achieve the benefits of competition and choice in ways that do not pose the same political risks to long-term funding levels that simple voucher systems could pose. The most obvious modification along these lines is a voucher system that targets only the most disadvantaged students. Under this approach, there is still a risk that the level of support offered though the voucher may be far too low to support the entry of entirely new providers of educational services. Even if the program begins with good intentions, it could easily end up resembling the Medicaid program. However, if this proposal did not have any adverse effect on the public school system, poor families could always return to the public schools if funding levels fell in the voucher-based system. In effect, it would be like giving the poor the option to be covered under either Medicaid or Medicare.

But even these targeted voucher systems pose a risk to existing public school systems. Now, it seems to be impossible to get a majority of voters to vote in a referendum for a switch to a voucher-based system that helps large numbers of middle- and upper-income families escape from the public schools. If a limited voucher system were in place, it might be possible to win a series of much-lower-profile legislative votes or administrative decisions, each of which expands the number of families that are eligible to collect the vouchers. Both sides in the political fight over targeted voucher programs for the poor seem to understand that what is being contested is not simply a program for poor children, but the initiation of a dynamic process that will ultimately move far beyond its initial focus.

It may seem excessively pessimistic to worry that political institutions in the United States will lead to an outcome in which children born into poor families receive schooling that in relative terms, and perhaps even in absolute terms, is even worse than it is now. However, one must take full account of the fact that virtually all the decent, ordinary citizens of the United States already are reconciled to the fact that there are millions of children throughout the world who receive abysmal levels of schooling, nutrition, and health care, and millions of children in the United States who fail to receive a level of medical care that is taken for granted in most developed countries of the world.

As a matter of pure logic, it is not clear why affluent voters should treat the disadvantaged children who live in the United States any differently from the disadvantaged children who live elsewhere in the world. In the abstract, it is not clear why they should support relative levels of spending for the education of rich and poor children in the United States that are more equal than relative levels of spending for medical care. Our current institutions force a level of interaction and exposure to a public school system that has important elements of commonality between the rich and poor in our own country. These institutions may force more equality in educational attainment than would prevail in their absence. Changes in our institutions could have a major impact on our commitment to education as a means of redistributing income within our nation.

Citizens of the United States who care about disadvantaged children living here have reason to fear that a move toward privatized education will lead in the future to less reliance on education as the mechanism for reducing income inequality. They recognize that the existing educational system is deeply flawed and serves students from disadvantaged backgrounds very badly. They are, nevertheless, correct that there is a substantial risk that existing proposals for privatization could significantly reduce the level of public funding for education at the same time that they generate true efficiency gains.

To persuade a majority of voters to embrace change, proponents of privatization should look much more carefully at the long-term effects that their proposals could have on levels of public funding for education. They should think more creatively about institutional mechanisms that could both capture the gains from privatization and preserve a broad political commitment to the use of education as a means of making progress toward our goal of giving every child from every family the chance to thrive in the economy of the future.

NOTES

1. Edward Lazear, "Intergenerational Externalities," *Canadian Journal of Economics* 16 (May 1983): 212–28.
2. Claudia Goldin and Lawrence F. Katz, "Technology, Skill, and the Wage Structure: Insights from the Past," *American Economic Review* 86, 2(1996): 252–57.
3. Claudia Goldin and Lawrence F. Katz, "The Origins of State-Level Differences in the Public Provision of Higher Education: 1890–1940," *American Economic Review* 88, 2(1998): 303–8. Claudia Goldin and Lawrence F. Katz, "The Origins of Technology-Skill Complementarity," *Quarterly Journal of Economics* 113, 3(1998): 693–732.
4. Lawrence Katz and Kevin Murphy, "Changes in Relative Wages, 1963–1987: Supply and Demand Factors," *Quarterly Journal of Economics* 107(1, 1992): 35–78.
5. OECD (Organization for Economic Cooperation and Development), "Literacy in the Age of Information. Final Report of the International Adult Literacy Survey," Paris 2000.

6. Stephen Norton, "Recent Trends in Medicaid Physician Fees, 1993–98," Urban Institute Discussion Paper 99-12, September 1999.

7. Paul Romer, "Preferences, Promises, and the Politics of Entitlement," in *Individual and Social Responsibility: Child Care, Education, Medical Care, and Long-Term Care in America*, ed. Victor R. Fuchs (Chicago: University of Chicago Press, 1995).

EDUCATION AND SOCIETY

The Education of Minority Children*

Thomas Sowell

Will Rogers once said that it was not ignorance that was so bad but, as he put it, "all the things we know that ain't so." Nowhere is that more true than in American education today, where fashions prevail and evidence is seldom asked or given. And nowhere does this do more harm than in the education of minority children.

The quest for esoteric methods of trying to educate these children proceeds as if such children had never been successfully educated before, when in fact there are concrete examples, both from history and from our times, of schools that have been successful in educating children from low-income families and from minority families.[1] Yet the educational dogma of the day is that you simply cannot expect children who are not middle-class to do well on standardized tests, for all sorts of sociological and psychological reasons.

Those who think this way are undeterred by the fact that there are schools where low-income and minority students do in fact score well on standardized tests. These students are like the bumblebees who supposedly should not be able

---

*Copyright © 2001 by Thomas Sowell

to fly, according to the theories of aerodynamics, but who fly anyway, in disregard of those theories.

While there are examples of schools where this happens in our own time—both public and private, secular and religious—we can also go back a hundred years and find the same phenomenon. Back in 1899, in Washington, D.C., there were four academic public high schools—one black and three white.[2] In standardized tests given that year, students in the black high school averaged higher test scores than students in two of the three white high schools.[3]

This was not a fluke. It so happens that I have followed eighty-five years of the history of this black high school—from 1870 to 1955—and found it repeatedly equaling or exceeding national norms on standardized tests. In the 1890s, it was called The M Street school and after 1916 it was renamed Dunbar High School, but its academic performances on standardized tests remained good on into the mid-1950s.

When I first published this information, more than twenty years ago, those few educators who responded at all dismissed the relevance of these findings by saying that these were "middle class" children and therefore their experience was not "relevant" to the education of low-income minority children. Those who said this had no factual data on the incomes or occupations of the parents of these children—and I did.

The problem, however, was not that these dismissive educators did not have evidence. The more fundamental problem was that they saw no *need* for evidence. According to their doctrines, children who did well on standardized tests were middle class. These children did well on such tests, therefore they were middle class.

Lack of evidence is not the problem. There was evidence on the occupations of the parents of the children at this school as far back as the early 1890s. As of academic year 1892-93, there were eighty-three known occupations of the parents of the children attending the M Street School. Of these occupations, fifty-one were laborers and *one* was a doctor.[4] That doesn't sound very middle class to me.

Over the years, a significant black middle class did develop in Washington and no doubt most of them sent their children to the M Street School or to Dunbar High School, as it was later called. But that is wholly different from saying that most of the children at that school came from middle-class homes.

During the later period, for which I collected data, there were far more children whose mothers were maids than there were whose fathers were doctors.[5] For many years, there was only one academic high school for blacks in the District of Columbia and, as late as 1948, one-third of all black youngsters attending high school in Washington attended Dunbar High School. So this was not a "selective" school in the sense in which we normally use that term there were no tests to take to get in, for example—even though there was undoubtedly *self-selection* in the sense that students who were serious went to Dunbar and those who were not had other places where they could while away their time, without having to meet high academic standards. (A vocational high school for blacks was opened in Washington in 1902.)[6]

A spot check of attendance records and tardiness records showed that The M Street School at the turn of the century and Dunbar High School at mid-century had less absenteeism and less tardiness than the white high schools in the District of Columbia at those times. The school had a tradition of being serious, going back to its founders and early principals.

Among these early principals was the first black woman to receive a college degree in the United States—Mary Jane Patterson—from Oberlin College, class of 1862. At that time, Oberlin had different academic curriculum requirements for women and men. Latin, Greek and mathematics were required in "the gentlemen's course," as it was called, but not in the curriculum for ladies. Miss Patterson, however, insisted on taking Latin, Greek, and mathematics anyway. Not surprisingly, in her later twelve years as principal of the black high school in Washington during its formative years, she was noted for "a strong, forceful personality," for "thoroughness," and for being "an indefatigable worker." Having this kind of person shaping the standards and traditions of the school in its early years undoubtedly had something to do with its later success.

Other early principals included the first black man to graduate from Harvard, class of 1870. Four of the school's first eight principals graduated from Oberlin and two from Harvard. Because of restricted academic opportunities for blacks, Dunbar had three Ph.Ds among its teachers as late as the 1920s.

One of the other educational dogmas of our times is the notion that standardized tests do not predict future performances for minority children, either in academic institutions or in life. Innumerable scholarly studies have devastated this claim intellectually,[7] though it still survives and flourishes politically.

But the history of this black high school in Washington likewise shows a pay-off for solid academic preparation and the test scores that result from it. Over the entire eighty-five-year history of academic success of this school, from 1870 to 1955, most of its 12,000 graduates went on to higher education.[8] This was very unusual for either black or white high-school graduates during this era. Because these were low-income students, most went to a local free teachers' college or to inexpensive Howard University,[9] but significant numbers won scholarships to leading colleges and universities elsewhere.

Some M Street School graduates began going away to academically elite colleges in the early twentieth century. In 1903, the first M Street graduate went to Harvard.[10] As of 1916, there were just nine black students, from the entire country, attending Amherst College. Six were from the M Street School. During the period from 1918 to 1923, graduates of this school went on to earn fifteen degrees from Ivy League colleges and another thirty-five degrees from other predominantly white institutions, including Amherst, Williams, and Wesleyan. This was in addition to 158 degrees from Howard University and hundreds of degrees from Miner Teachers College in Washington, both these institutions being predominantly black.[11] Over the period from 1892 to 1954, Amherst admitted thirty-four graduates of the M Street School and Dunbar. Of these, seventy-four percent graduated and more than one-fourth of these graduates were Phi Beta Kappas.[12]

No systematic study has been made of the later careers of the graduates of this school. However, when the late black educator Horace Mann Bond studied the backgrounds of blacks with Ph.D.s, he discovered that more of them had graduated from M Street-Dunbar than from any other black high school in the country.

The first blacks to graduate from West Point and Annapolis also came from this school. So did the first black full professor at a major university (Allison Davis at the University of Chicago). So did the first black federal judge, the first black general, the first black Cabinet member, the first black elected to the United States Senate since Reconstruction, and the discoverer of blood plasma. During World War II, when black military officers were rare, there were more than two dozen graduates of M Street or Dunbar High School holding ranks ranging from major to brigadier general.[13]

All this contradicts another widely-believed notion—that schools do not make much difference in children's academic or career success because income and family background are much larger influences. If the schools do not differ very much from one another, then of course it will not make much difference which one a child attends. But, when they differ dramatically, the results can also differ dramatically.

This was not the only school to achieve success with minority children. But, before turning to some other examples, it may be useful to consider why and how this eighty-five-year history of unusual success was abruptly turned into typical failure, almost overnight, by the politics of education.

As we all know, 1954 was the year of the famous racial desegregation case of *Brown v. Board of Education*. Those of us old enough to remember those days also know of the strong resistance to school desegregation in many white communities, including Washington, D.C. Ultimately a political compromise was worked out. In order to comply with the law, without having a massive shift of students, the District's school officials decided to turn all Washington public schools into neighborhood schools.

By this time, the neighborhood around Dunbar High School was rundown. This had not affected the school's academic standards, however, because black students from all over the city went to Dunbar, but very few of those who lived in its immediate vicinity did.

When Dunbar became a neighborhood school, the whole character of its student body changed radically—and the character of its teaching staff changed very soon afterward. In the past, many Dunbar teachers continued to teach for years after they were eligible for retirement because it was such a fulfilling experience. Now, as inadequately educated, inadequately motivated, and disruptive students flooded into the school, teachers began retiring, some as early as fifty-five years of age. Inside of a very few years, Dunbar became just another failing ghetto school, with all the problems that such schools have, all across the country. Eighty-five years of achievement simply vanished into thin air.

It is a very revealing fact about the politics of education that no one tried to stop this from happening. When I first began to study the history of this school, back in the 1970s, I thought that it was inconceivable that this could have been allowed to happen without a protest. I knew that the Washington school board in the 1950s included a very militant and distinguished black woman named Margaret Just Butcher, who was also a graduate of Dunbar High school. Surely Dr. Butcher had not let all this happen without exercising her well-known gifts of withering criticism.

Yet I looked in vain through the minutes of the school board for even a single sentence by anybody expressing any concern whatever about the fate of Dunbar High School under the new reorganization plan. Finally, in complete frustration and bewilderment, I phoned Dr. Butcher herself. Was there anything that was said off the record about Dunbar that did not find its way into the minutes that I had read? "No," she said. Then she reminded me that racial "integration" was the battle cry of the hour in the 1950s. No one thought about what would happen to black schools, not even Dunbar.

Now, decades later, we still do not have racial integration in many of the urban schools around the country—and we also do not have Dunbar High School. Such are the ways of politics, where the crusade of the hour often blocks out everything else, at least until another crusade comes along and takes over the same monopoly of our minds.

Ironically, black high schools in Washington today have many of the so-called "prerequisites" for good education that never existed in the heyday of Dunbar High School and yet the educational results are abysmal. "Adequate funding" is always included among these "prerequisites" and today the per pupil expenditure in the District of Columbia is among the highest in the nation. During its heyday, Dunbar was starved for funds and its average class size was in the 40s. Its lunchroom was so small that many of its students had to eat out on the streets. Its blackboards were cracked and it was 1950 before the school had a public address system. Yet, at that point, it had eighty years of achievement behind it—and only five more in front of it.

As a failing ghetto school today, Dunbar has a finer physical plant than it ever had when it was an academic success. Politics is also part of this picture. Immediate, tangible symbols are what matter within the limited time horizon of elected politicians. Throwing money at public schools produces such symbolic results, even if it cannot produce quality education.

Another black school that I studied—P.S. 91 in Brooklyn, New York—was housed in an even older building than the original Dunbar High School. This building in Brooklyn was so old that it still had gas jets in the hallways, left over from the gaslight era, before there were electric lights. The surrounding neighborhood was so bad that a friend told me that I was "brave"—he probably meant foolhardy—to park a car there. Yet the students in most of the grades in this predominantly black elementary school scored at or above the national norms on standardized tests.

This was not in any sense a middle-class school or a magnet school. It was just an ordinary ghetto school run by an extraordinary principal. What was more extraordinary to me than even the test scores of the students was the openness with which I was welcomed and allowed to see what I wanted to see.

Educators usually like to give guided tours to selected (and often atypical) places, much like the Potemkin village tours in Czarist Russia. But, in P.S. 92, I was allowed to wander down the halls and arbitrarily pick out which classrooms I wanted to go into. I did this on every floor of the school.

Inside these classrooms were black children much like children you can find in any ghetto across the country. Many came from broken homes and were on welfare. Yet, inside this school, they spoke in grammatical English, in complete sentences, and to the point. Many of the materials they were studying were a year or more ahead of their respective grade levels.

It so happened that I had to fly back to California right after visiting this school and did not get to talk to all the people I wanted to interview. I asked a mother who was head of the school's Parent-Teacher Association if I could call her at home after I got back to California and interview her over the phone. It turned out that she did not have a telephone. "I can't afford one," she said. That too hardly seemed middle class.

Others have found successful black schools operating in equally grim surroundings and under similar social conditions including a whole school district in Los Angeles.[14] Back in the 1970s, I studied two academically successful Catholic schools with black students in New Orleans. In both schools, a majority of the parental occupations were in the "unskilled and semi-skilled" category. Last year Dr. Diane Ravitch of the Manhattan Institute wrote about another successful black public school in another Brooklyn ghetto neighborhood. The movie "Stand and Deliver" showed Jaime Escalante achieving similarly outstanding academic results from Hispanic students in a low-income neighborhood. Yet the dogma marches on that a middle-class background is necessary for academic success.

St. Augustine high school in New Orleans was a particularly striking example of achieving academic success while going against the grain of prevailing opinion in educational circles. It was established back in 1951, during the era of racial segregation in the South, as a school for black boys, presided over by an all-white staff from the Josephite order. None of these young priests had ever taken a course in a department or school of education. To the horror of some outside members of the order, the school used corporal punishment. There was no unifying educational theory. The school kept doing things that worked and discarded things that didn't.

The first black student from the South to win a National Merit Scholarship came from St. Augustine. So did the first Presidential Scholar of any race from the state of Louisiana. As of 1974, 20 percent of all Presidential Scholars in the history of the state had come from this school with about 600 black students.

Test scores were never used as a rigid cutoff for admission to St. Augustine. There were students there with I.Q.s in the 60s, as well as others with I.Q.s more than twice that high. For individual students and for the school as a whole, the average I.Q. rose over the years being in the 80s and 90s in the 1950s and then reaching the national average of 100 in the 1960s. To put that in perspective, both blacks and whites in the South during this era tended to score below the national average on I.Q. and other standardized tests.

Most of these children did not come from middle-class families. Those whose parents were in professional or white-collar occupations were less than one-tenth as numerous as those whose parents worked in "unskilled and semi-skilled" occupations.

What are the "secrets" of such successful schools?

The biggest secret is that there are no secrets, unless work is a secret. Work seems to be the only four-letter word that cannot be used in public today.

Aside from work and discipline, the various successful schools for minority children have had little in common with one another and even less in common with the fashionable educational theories of our times. Some of these schools were public, some were private. Some were secular and some were religious. Dunbar High School had an all-black teaching staff but St. Augustine in New Orleans began with an all-white teaching staff. Some of these schools were housed in old run-down buildings and others in new, modern facilities. Some of their principals were finely attuned to the social and political nuances, while others were blunt people who could not have cared less about such things and would have failed Public Relations One.

None of these successful schools had a curriculum especially designed for blacks. Most had some passing recognition of the children's backgrounds. Dunbar High School, for example, was named for black poet Paul Laurence Dunbar and it set aside one day a year to commemorate Frederick Douglass, but its curriculum could hardly be called Afrocentric. Throughout the eighty-five years of its academic success, it taught Latin. In some of the early years, it taught Greek as well. Its whole focus was on expanding the students' cultural horizons, not turning their minds inward.

For all I know, there may be some Afrocentric schools that are doing well. The point here is simply that this has not been an essential ingredient in the successful education of minority students. At St. Augustine school in New Orleans, its principal, Father Grant, resisted attempts to bring into the school the issues arising from the civil rights struggles of the 1960s. Although sympathetic to the civil rights movement himself, and to some extent a participant in it, Father Grant opposed the introduction into the school of what he called "extraneous elements, issues, and concerns." Keenly aware of the students' cultural disadvantages and the need to overcome them, as well as the importance of the social issues that some wanted to address in the school, he said that "we absolutely could not do both things well"—and both deserved to be done well or not at all. As Father grant put it bluntly: "Do not consume my time with extraneous issues and then expect me to have enough time left over to dedicate myself to a strong academic program where I will turn out strong, intelligent, competent kids."

Again, the point here is not to say that this is the only viable approach. The point is that the social visions of the day have not been essential ingredients in educational success.

Important as the history of outstanding schools for minority students has been, there is also much to learn from the history of very ordinary urban ghetto schools, which often did far better in the past—both absolutely and relative to their white contemporaries than is the case today. I went to such schools in Harlem in the 1940s but I do not rely on nostalgia for my information. The test scores in ordinary Harlem schools in the 1940s were quite comparable to the test scores in white working-class neighborhoods on New York's lower east side.

Sometimes the Harlem schools scored a little higher and sometimes the lower east side schools scored little higher but there were no such glaring racial disparities as we have become used to in urban schools in recent years. In April, 1941, for example, some lower east side schools scored slightly higher on tests of word meaning and paragraph meaning than some schools in Harlem but, in tests given in December of that same year, several Harlem schools scored higher than the lower east side schools. Neither set of schools scored as high as the city-wide average, though neither was hopelessly below it.[15]

While the lower east side of New York is justly known for the many people who were born in poverty there and rose to middle-class levels—and some to national prominence—very little attention is paid to a very similar history in Harlem. Some years ago, a national magazine ran a flattering profile of me, expressing wonder that I had come out of Harlem and gone on to elite colleges and an academic career.

Shortly thereafter, I received a letter from a black lawyer of my generation, pointing out that my experience was by no means so unusual in those days. He had grown up in Harlem during the same era, just a few blocks from me. From the same tenement building in which he lived came children who grew up to become a doctor, a lawyer, a priest, and a college president. Indeed, where did today's black middle class come from, it not from such places and such schools? My great fear is that a black child growing up in Harlem today will not have as good a chance to rise as people of my generation did, simply because they will not receive as solid an education, in an era when such an education is even more important.

Parents have been an important ingredient in the success of schools, whatever the racial or social backgrounds of the students. But the specific nature of parental involvement can vary greatly—and has often been very different from what is believed among some educational theorists. In some of the most successful schools, especially of the past, the parents' role has been that of giving moral support to the school by letting their children know that they are expected to learn and to behave themselves.

Current educational fashions see parents' roles as that of active participants in the shaping of educational policy and on-site involvement in the daily activities of the schools. Whatever the merits or demerits of these notions, that was certainly not the role played by parents of children at successful schools in the past. Nor were they necessarily equipped to play such a role. As of 1940, for example, the average black adult in the United States had only an elementary school education. I can still remember being surprised at what an event it was in our family when I was promoted to the seventh grade—because no one else in the family had ever gone that far before.

It was much the same story on the lower east side of New York at that time. Biographies of immigrant children who grew up there are full of painful memories of how their parents, with their meager education and broken English, hated to have to go see a teacher—and how embarrassed their children were when their parents appeared at school.

Parents today may be more educated and more sophisticated but it is not clear that their political or quasi-political involvement in schools has been a net benefit. At the very least, history shows that it has never been essential.

For those who are interested in schools that produce academic success for minority students, there is no lack of examples, past and present. Tragically, there is a lack of interest by the public school establishment in such examples. Again, I think this goes back to the politics of education.

Put bluntly, failure attracts more money than success. Politically, failure becomes a reason to demand more money, smaller classes, and more trendy courses and programs, ranging from "black English" to bilingualism and "self-esteem." Politicians who want to look compassionate and concerned know that voting money for such projects accomplishes that purpose for them and voting against such programs risks charges of mean-spiritedness, if not implications of racism.

We cannot recapture the past and there is much in the past that we should not want to recapture. But neither is it irrelevant. If nothing else, history shows what can be achieved, even in the face of adversity. We have no excuse for achieving less in an era of greater material abundance and greater social opportunities.

NOTES

1. See for example, Samuel Casey Carter. *No Excuses: Lessons from Twenty-One High Performing, High-Poverty Schools.* (Washington: The Heritage Foundation, 2000); Duke Helfland. "Inglewood Writes the Book on Success." *Los Angeles Times,* April 30, 2000: A1 ff; Thomas Sowell, "Patterns of Black Excellence." *The Public Interest,* Spring 1976: 26–58.
2. *Report of the Board of Trustees of Public Schools of the District of Columbia to the Commissioners of the District of Columbia: 1898–1899.* (Washington: Government Printing Office, 1900): 7, 11.

3. Henry S. Robinson. "The M Street School." *Records of the Columbia Historical Society of Washington, D.C.*, Vol. LI (1984): 122; Constance Green, *The Secret City: A History of Race Relations in the Nation's Capital.* (Princeton: Princeton University Press, 1967): 137.
4. Ibid., 141.
5. Detailed data on these students, including their parents' occupations, can be obtained from National Technical Information Service, U.S. Department of Commerce, Springfield, Virginia 22161. (Accession Number PB265 8.13).
6. Constance Green, *The Secret City*, 168.
7. See the numerous references listed in Thomas Sowell. *Inside American Education.* (New York: The Free Press, 1993); 322, footnote 99.
8. Mary Gibson Hundley. *The Dunbar Story* (1870–1955). (New York: Vantage Press, 1965): 24, 61.
9. Ibid., 147.
10. Henry S. Robinson. "The M Street School." *Records of the Columbia Historical Society of Washington, D.C.*, Vol. LI (1984): 122.
11. Mary Gibson Hundley, *The Dunbar Story*, 149–150.
12. Ibid., 75.
13. Ibid., 57.
14. Duke Helfland. "Inglewood Writes the Book on Success." *Los Angeles Times*, April 30, 2000: A1 ff.
15. See data shown in Thomas Sowell. "Assumptions versus History in Ethnic Education." *Teachers College Record.*, Vol. 83, No. 1 (Fall 1981): 40–41

Educating Black Students

Shelby Steele

The problems surrounding the education of America's black youth are usually presumed to follow from either racism or poverty or both. America's terrible racial history adds a compelling logic to this presumption, and no doubt poverty remains a profound problem even if racism is far less a problem than it once was. But I believe that something very different from these two familiar difficulties is undermining the academic development of today's black youth. Allow me to begin with a speculation.

Suppose America decided that black people were poor in music because of deprivations due to historical racism. Clearly their improvement in this area would be contingent on the will of white America to intervene on their behalf. Surely well-designed interventions would enable blacks to close the musical gap with whites. Imagine that in one such program a young, reluctant, and disengaged Charlie Parker is being tutored in the saxophone by a college student.

The tutor learns that Parker's father drank too much and abandoned the family, and that his mother has had an affair with a married man. Young Charlie is often late to his tutorial sessions. Secretly the tutor comes to feel that probably his real purpose is therapeutic, because the terrible circumstances of Charlie's life make it highly unlikely that he will ever be focused enough to master the complex keying system of the saxophone or learn to read music competently. The tutor says as much in a lonely, late-night call to his own father, who tells him in a supportive tone that in this kind of work the results one works for are not always the important ones. If Charlie doesn't learn the saxophone, it doesn't mean that he isn't benefiting from the attention. Also, the father says, "What pleases me is how much you are growing as a human being."

And Charlie smiles politely at his tutor but secretly feels that the tutor's pained attentions are evidence that he, Charlie, must be inadequate in some way. He finds it harder to pay attention during his lessons. He has also heard from many that the saxophone—a European instrument—really has little to do with who he is. He tells this to the tutor one day after a particularly poor practice session. The tutor is sympathetic because he, too, has recently learned that it is not exactly esteem building to impose a European instrument on an African-American child.

Finally Charlie stops coming to the program. The tutor accepts this failure as inevitable. Sadly, he realizes that he had been expecting it all along. But he misses Charlie, and for the first time he feels a genuine anger at his racist nation, a nation that has bred such discouragement into black children. The young tutor realizes that surely Charlie could have been saved had there been a program to intervene earlier in his life. And for the first time in his life the tutor understands the necessity for political involvement. He redoubles his commitment to an America that works "proactively" to transform and uplift its poor, and that carries out this work with genuine respect for cultural differences.

The following fall, back at college, he says in amazement to his favorite history professor, "Can you imagine? Teaching saxophone to a poor black kid from Kansas City?"

Of course the true story of Charlie Parker is quite different from this. Though he did grow up poor, black, and fatherless in the depression, he also became the greatest improvisational saxophone player in the history of music. When he died far too young at the age of thirty-five, he had already changed Western music forever.

Why was Charlie Parker, along with thousands and thousands of other blacks (few of whom were geniuses on a par with him), so successful at the high and complex art form of jazz despite suffering the same litany of deprivations that is today used to explain the weak academic performance of black students? Throughout the 1990s, the academic gap between blacks and whites widened, when every objective circumstance suggested that it should have narrowed. Worse, several studies including one by the American College Board tell us that this gap is wider between middle-class blacks and whites than it is between poor blacks and whites. This refutes the conventional wisdom that has always seen economic deprivation as the culprit in poor academic performance among blacks.

No other student group in America (and possibly the entire world) has been more studied and had its academic weaknesses more analyzed than black American students. No group has had more special programs created on its behalf or more educational theories generated in its name. And today there is no student group whose performance is more fretted over than black students. There is even an unspoken assumption that this group's performance is an indication of the moral health of the society.

Yet the general picture of black academic performance is nothing less than terrible. Black students at every age and grade level generally perform worse than all other groups on virtually every academic measure—test scores, grades, school attendance levels, drop-out rates, suspension rates, and so on. Black college students have the lowest collective grade point average and the highest collective drop-out rate of all student groups. And throughout the 1990s the notorious academic gap between black and white students (SAT scores are one obvious measure) only widened, despite the fact that it had been narrowing a little during the 1970s and 1980s.

It is the relentlessness, the seeming insistence on academic weakness in black students that mystifies. I think at least part of the explanation for this can be seen in the story of the real Charlie Parker—a man who came from an area of life where black performance has always been superb rather than terrible.

I believe the real Charlie Parker had two profound advantages over his fictional counterpart. The first was that the America he lived in did not care at all about his musical development. During the depression there were no programs or tutors devoted to black musical development. In this void of indifference there was nothing between Charlie and his saxophone. Maybe he heard the music of a great musician such as Lester Young or Ben Webster and was deeply moved. However he came to the alto saxophone, the disinterest of the society in his playing allowed him to relate directly to the business of making music. There was no subtext for him to decipher as he worked at the instrument, no intimations of guilt in the larger society toward him, and no sense that his achievement might have a social and political significance. He was simply a young boy with an instrument who wanted to make music. As his commitment to the instrument deepened, he had no trouble setting himself to the hard work and long hours of practice that mastery required.

The second great advantage was evident after Charlie became very good on his instrument. Wanting to show off his new talent, he sat in on a jam session with a visiting band— a common practice among black musicians then and now. After he played long enough for the professionals to get a measure of his skills, the drummer dislodged a cymbal from his drum set and threw it at Charlie. Like the infamous hook in the theater, it was the sign to get off stage and go back to the "woodshed," the metaphorical crucible in which musicians develop their craft. So Charlie's second great advantage was that he belonged to a community in which only excellence was acceptable—a community that enforced excellence as an impersonal standard. The drummer was not humiliating Charlie so much as pointing to the bar of excellence. These two advantages—the disinterest of the larger society and an impersonal devotion to excellence in his own community—made Charlie's economic deprivations virtually irrelevant to his achievement. In this "clean" environment his deprivation was only a prod; it excused him from nothing.

But does this mean that the social program and the tutor were actual disadvantages for the fictional Charlie? I think so. The tutor let his idea of Charlie's deprivations move him to an unexamined faith that concern was the true ingredient missing from Charlie's life. If the tutor could show concern, if America could overcome its intractable indifference toward blacks and become concerned about their uplift, if people could consider mentoring, if educational funding could be more equitably distributed, if. . . . The mistake in this faith is that it makes the concern of others the agent of black social transformation. In this faith blacks are conceived as essentially inert people so overcome by deprivation that only the concerned intervention of others can transform them into self-sufficient people. Others act; blacks are acted upon. This is a profound mistake with a litany of terrible consequences for blacks. It encourages this people coming up from three centuries of oppression to trade away agency over their own advancement in order to gain the help of others. Worse, it encourages them to argue their own weakness in order to qualify for such help. It puts them in the same position as the fictional Charlie—looking to a "tutor" who is inept and self-absorbed rather than to their own talents and energies.

What is agency? It is ultimate responsibility combined with possession. You have agency over something—a life, a problem, an education—when you have the freedom that allows you to be responsible for it and when you accept that this responsibility belongs to you whether or not others support you.

Many families in America want their children to become well educated, and they are willing to do what is necessary to agent that goal. They read to them in early childhood. They ask for their thoughts in frequent and pleasant conversations. They take them places and teach them to respond to the larger world. And then, having consciously nurtured their child's mind, having understood this to be an important part of parenting, they try to arrange schooling that will continue this process, schooling that is safe and challenging. If the local public school does not offer this, they will go elsewhere to find it. They will move to a better school district or pay for a private school or even try home schooling because they understand that a poor local school does not excuse them from the responsibility of providing a good education for their children. Circumstances can surely limit what even the most responsible family can achieve, but no family is ever really excused from the responsibility of imaginatively fighting difficult circumstances. President Clinton, of course, showed this kind of agency when he sent his daughter to a private school. As the responsible agent of his daughter's education, he simply chose an elite private education over a poor public one in the schools of Washington, D.C. I would have done the same thing. Agency involves determination and commitment. The real Charlie Parker withstood the ire of his neighbors who complained of his constant practicing. President Clinton withstood the political fallout that came to him as a Democratic President seemingly scorning the public schools when it came to his own daughter.

A recent study from the Manhattan Institute (Education Freedom Index) found that academic achievement was higher in states where more "educational freedom" prevailed. In states such as Arizona and Minnesota, where there are many charter schools to choose from and where home schooling is allowed, SAT and NAEP (National Assessment of Educational Progress) scores were significantly higher than in states such as Hawaii and West Virginia, where charter schools and home schooling are discouraged or heavily regulated. Could it be that the more "educationally free" states encourage their parents to be the responsible agents of their children's educations? Or maybe the demand for more agency by parents in some states leads to freer educational policies.

The point is that there is an indisputable relationship between agency and excellence and that black America—as with all other communities—performs well wherever it sees itself as the responsible agent and performs poorly wherever it doesn't. Agency is a call to the will, a demand that we find the will even if our circumstances are bleak, even if great sacrifices are required. Because agency is so demanding, it has to be supported by an entire constellation of values that today would be called "traditional," a commitment to excellence, hard work, delayed gratification, initiative, risk-taking, etc. Among other things these values organize and focus the will. Agency is not really possible without them. Or conversely, agency always makes these values necessary.

It is certainly true that poverty and racism can affect how well a group performs in a given area. But it is also true that poverty and even racism do not prevent a group from achieving excellence when it takes agency over an area and begins to live by the values that allow the will to be applied. Charlie Parker was one of thousands of black Americans who made a living in music even while segregation was pervasive. Obviously this does not mean that segregation was a benign or tolerable institution. It merely points to the relationship between group agency and group performance. American minority groups that have taken agency over their educational performance—Jews and many Asian-American groups are obvious examples—have done in education what blacks have done in music. They have excelled.

The first sign that a group (race, ethnic group, tribe, nationality, gender, region, etc.) has taken agency over an area is that it impersonally enforces a rigorous standard of excellence. Somehow the group decides that its future or even its survival depend on its performance in a given area. Soon it begins to esteem individuals who perform well in those areas. This does not mean that others are devalued, only that those who perform well are seen as special carriers of group pride and honor. Achievement is reinforced by the group bestowing special esteem on its high-performing members. And in group lore this high performance is presumed to result from a special genius that is unique to the group. Thus, Charlie Parker's musical greatness was seen to come from a special black genius, and he was rewarded with much esteem from his group.

When a group takes agency in an area, it evolves an "identity" legend or mythology that in effect says, "we do such-and-such very well"—"we sing well," "we are smart," "we know business," etc. The group presumes itself excellent in the area it takes agency over and then rewards individuals for manifesting this excellence that is now said to be inherent to the group. People grow up in the knowledge that their group excels in certain areas and that their membership (identity) in the group may give them special potential in these areas.

Of course, once this self-fulfilling prophecy is set in motion, the group will likely become excellent in the area it has taken agency over. And from this achievement it also begins to build very real expertise in this area that can be continually refined and passed on within the group. So there is a movement from agency to a priori faith to achievement to evolving expertise.

In some cases excellence no doubt shows itself before the group takes agency. Maybe there were many superb black singers before the group claimed an inherent excellence in this area. But this is only a chicken-or-egg argument. Agency—a level of responsibility in which the group proudly and fearlessly enforces impersonal standards of excellence in an area as a statement of group identity—must happen for a group to perform competitively in an area over time.

Group identities are constructed out of agency by what a group takes responsibility for and by the degree of that responsibility. Despite poverty and intractable segregation, the real Charlie Parker succeeded because he developed his talent in an area that was at the center of his group's identity. The extraordinary power of this identity-agency paradigm is evident today in the multi-billion-dollar rap music industry, an industry created and sustained by the very same deprived inner-city blacks who perform so terribly in school.

Of course, group identities are not shaped in a vacuum. In Parker's day music was open to blacks but neurosurgery was not. Music could be learned and practiced without a higher education; medicine could not be. Oppressed minorities, in effect, have always negotiated with a hostile larger society over where they could invest the group identity by taking agency. In today's world this negotiation is no longer necessary. In America groups can take agency anywhere they wish. They can remold their identity at will. Individuals can select wider circles of identity than the traditional groups they are born into and take agency wherever they see possibility. Today's America is a fluid society with little restriction on the assumption of agency beyond the individual imagination.

This said, I believe this identity-agency paradigm still affects the performance profile of black Americans. Group identity is very strong in this group, which means that the group's taking or rejecting of agency is more determining of performance than it might be in other groups. Black America now practices identity politics more intensely than any other group in American life. Conforming to the group's selection of agency wins one an esteemed identity; nonconformity puts one's group identity in great jeopardy. So it is no accident that the academic performance of black students is so weak today. The group has not taken agency over the academic development of its children in the way that it has taken agency over their development in other areas. One remarkable indication of this is the fact that excellent black students from middle school to college are often taunted as "white wannabes." This constitutes nothing less than a tragic irony: the esteemed identity goes to the weak black student and is denied to the high-achieving black student. The excellent student is denied a feeling of belonging and esteem from his group. He is made to suffer isolation and alienation for his academic excellence.

I must add here that wider America has also not taken agency over the academic development of black children. No one has. For the last thirty-five years, neither black America nor wider America enforced rigorous standards of academic excellence for black youth. Less and less has been asked of black students and weaker-and-weaker performance has been allowed to count for them—social promotion in K-12 and lower standards for college admission than for other groups. The struggle by universities across the country to keep affirmative action is also, inadvertently, a struggle to keep admission standards lower for blacks, to continue the practice of asking less of them than of others. No group in American society has been more betrayed by American education over the past thirty-five years than black American young people. It is now clear that the primary device for treating their academic weakness has been to grant them a license to academic mediocrity. I have written elsewhere about the peculiar symbiosis of black anger and white guilt that this blindness to simple human need was born of. Suffice it to say here (in a bit of an oversimplification) that whites have had to prove themselves innocent of racism by supporting programs of lowered expectations and double standards for blacks. Blacks understandably developed a sense of entitlement that became a part of their group identity. What happened quite unintentionally is that both groups took agency for black weakness rather than for black strength. Both groups needed the weakness more than the strength in their symbiotic trading. Without black weakness how could America redeem its moral authority from its shameful history of racism? And, if blacks were strong academically, how could they get the programs and money that are a proxy for historical justice? Untold billions of government and private dollars have been spent since the 1960s in the name of black disadvantage. Millions of careers have developed and flourished. Black academic success would end the flow of these dollars and destroy the rationale for these careers.

So when educators sit down to consider how to improve the achievement of black students, they are dealing with a group that is, at the very least, ambivalent about taking agency over the education of its young people—this despite all its vociferous claims to the contrary. In fact, this group inadvertently protects the academic weakness and mediocrity of its youth as a way of sustaining its entitlement. It uses group identity more to punish academic excellence than to punish academic weakness. The weak achiever is the true black; the high achiever is a white wannabe.

Educators today must understand that the group identity of their black students—as currently constructed—is very likely a barrier to the educational disciplines that high academic achievement requires. It may be impossible for educators to entirely overcome a barrier this profound. Group identity is strong in all people and stronger still in blacks. And as long as wider America continues to use black weakness as the occasion to pay off an historical debt, the incentive lies with weakness rather than with strength.

Still, the challenge for today's educators is to do what the black identity is currently failing to do: to enforce for black students at all levels a strict and impersonal accountability to the highest standards of excellence. The challenge is to stand before that poor black student from a single-parent home and a drug-infested neighborhood and ask more than is asked of his wealthy white counterpart in a suburban private school. This is agency. This is the difference between the fictional and the real Charlie Parker.

Delivering Education

Andrew J. Coulson

Our system of education . . . is to be contrasted with our highest ideas of perfection itself. . . . The love of excellence looks ever upward towards a higher standard; it is unimproving pride and arrogance only, that are satisfied with being superior to a lower [standard].—HORACE MANN

Horace Mann, father of U.S. public schooling, campaigned for the kind of education system he believed would best serve our children and our society. He did not simply seek improvements in the status quo, he sought excellence. That standard of excellence is rarely seen today. In our contemporary debate over school choice, we have succumbed to precisely the unimproving pride and arrogance against which Mann railed. We no longer ask what is the best approach to educating our children, we ask only how we can minimize the flaws in our current approach. We talk always of "reform" and never of rebirth. But our children are no less worthy of a commitment to excellence than were the children of Mann's time, and we cannot allow another generation to be sacrificed to our own complacency and lack of vision. We must throw off our blinders and strive to build the best education system we can.

The first step in that effort is to define the criteria by which the best systems can be identified. What, in other words, do we expect from our schools? Using polls, focus groups, and voting patterns as a guide,[1] it is possible to distinguish two categories of expectations: the individual and the social. In the first category are the things parents want for their own children, and in the second are the broader social effects we all want our educational system to produce. For parents, preparation for success in life and work is paramount, and specific goals include such things as mastery of basic academic and job skills, moral/religious education, a safe/studious educational setting, and the desire that these can be achieved affordably. There is considerable agreement among parents on the importance of job skills and basic academics, but preferences vary dramatically in other areas, especially with respect to religious instruction. To satisfy all families, an educational system must be able to cater to these differences. Our social goals, essentially the ideals of public education, include the following: that all children should have access to a good education regardless of income, that our schools should foster social harmony, that they should encourage parental involvement and responsibility, and that they should promote understanding of, and participation in, the democratic process.

The aforementioned goals provide a yardstick by which to measure educational systems, so our next step is to find alternative systems to measure. The two most common suggestions are to use analogies to other industries or to look at existing small-scale experiments with government-funded vouchers. These are both objects worthy of our attention, but they do have shortcomings. Arguments based on analogy are susceptible to many criticisms because of their theoretical nature. It is often contended, for instance, that educators and education are sufficiently different from other workers and industries that they do not bear comparison. Voucher experiments are usually so small that there are serious questions as to their generalizability. Also troubling is the fact that existing voucher programs do not actually represent the sort of model that they are sometimes purported to test. Vouchers are often said to create freely competitive education markets, but in fact can be highly restrictive (for example, by excluding religious schools), and they separate payment from consumption through a single-payer system, grossly distorting normal market incentives. One such distortion is that voucher-redeeming schools can lobby the state to increase their profits, rather than being obliged to either offer better services to customers (for which they could charge more) or to deliver their services more efficiently.

Where else, then, can we look for alternatives to the status quo? One rarely followed avenue is to study how the educational systems of other nations are organized and how well they seem to be working. While most countries have state-run school systems fundamentally similar to our own, there are some remarkable exceptions. Another approach is to ask how the civilizations that preceded ours saw to the education of their children. Children are not a recent invention, and formal education has been widely practiced for 2,500 years. As it turns out, the educational systems of our ancestors have much to teach us.

In considering the international and historical evidence, however, we are faced with a problem: how do we make sense of and compare education systems operating in vastly different times and places? A careful strategy is needed for sifting through the precedents and separating meaningful trends from spurious aberrations. My own strategy has been to turn the great variations among cultures into an advantage by combining the results of the following three kinds of investigations:

• Observe how similar school systems operate across many different cultural, technological, and economic settings.

• Observe how different school systems operate in similar settings.

• Observe changes in outcomes that occur as a particular society moves from one educational system to another.

Distilled to its simplest, the argument is that systems that have consistently produced good results across many different times and places are likely to have inherent advantages over systems that have consistently produced bad results regardless of their settings. Of course, conclusions drawn using this strategy will still generate debate, but, unlike the current battles over school choice, that debate can be focused on hard evidence, allowing us to advance our understanding of the kinds of school systems that serve the public well, the kinds that don't, and the reasons for the discrepancies.

The education systems examined in this study were chosen to ensure coverage of a wide range of cultures and time periods. Schools from ancient Greece, to the early medieval Islamic empire, to the modern United States and Japan, among others, are all discussed. Of special interest are the cases for which strong claims have been made by previous historians and scholars of education. The rise of fully tax-funded public schooling in the nineteenth-century United States, for instance, is often credited with bringing literacy and learning to the masses who would not otherwise have enjoyed them. Similarly, the modern state school system of Japan is widely regarded as a model for other nations, due to the strong academic performance of its students on international tests. Also, note that some significant chapters of human history, such as medieval Europe, are omitted from consideration because formal education simply did not reach the masses of the people.[2]

What follows is a brief distillation of the study just described, which was published in its entirety as *Market Education: The Unknown History*. The findings are presented topically, based on the individual and social goals described earlier.

ACADEMIC ACHIEVEMENT AND JOB PREPARATION

Horace Mann and his successors predicted that centralizing decision-making in the hands of state-appointed experts would lead to great improvements in pedagogy and hence in academic outcomes. This has not turned out to be the case. Public school systems have in fact tended to select teaching methods and materials arbitrarily, rather than relying on evidence of their effectiveness. More generally, government-run schools have not done as good a job of delivering the sort of academic instruction parents want as have free educational markets.

In the 1930s, the most time-tested technique for early reading instruction fell out of fashion[3]—not because it was ineffective, but because it was incompatible with the prevalent "progressive" education philosophy. Intensive phonics lessons, in which children had been taught to recognize words by sounding out their constituent parts, were felt to be too structured, confining, and teacher-directed. Leading educational theorists such as Francis Parker, G. Stanley Hall, and the still-famous John Dewey identified instead with the spirit-of-the-"word" method, in which children were expected to memorize whole words by sight. This memorization was to take place incidental to the reading process, however, and not through drill and repetition of words in isolation.

Progressive educators believed that children should be released from what they perceived as the straitjacket of traditional schooling and set free to explore learning in their own way. Organized and teacher-directed classes in letter-sound correspondences simply didn't fit this bill, so the most influential voices in education came down squarely in favor of the word method, and public schools soon fell into line behind them.

What is most remarkable about this pedagogical sea change is that it had no grounding in empirical research. There were no rigorous classroom trials demonstrating that the word method did a better job than phonics in teaching young children how to read. More than that, some proponents of the word method seemed indifferent to the relative effectiveness of the two methods, placing far greater emphasis on the teaching process itself than on its results. The word method was not preferred over phonics because it was believed to teach reading more quickly or successfully, but because it led to less structured, more pleasant-seeming lessons. For Stanley Hall, who advocated that reading and writing "should be neglected in our system before [age] eight[4]", learning to read was itself greatly overrated:

> Very many men have lived and died and been great, even the leaders of their age, without any acquaintance with letters. The knowledge which illiterates acquire is probably on the whole more personal, direct, environmental and probably a much larger proportion of it practical. Moreover, they escape much eyestrain and mental excitement.[5]

Hall even cited famous illiterates, such as the eighth-century emperor Charlemagne, to underscore his point. Ironically, Charlemagne was a vigorous proponent of spreading literacy to the masses, and tried hard to learn to read and write in what little spare time he could find.[6] These noisome historical details appear to have been lost on Hall.

Since the 1930s, a large body of evidence has developed showing the superiority of reading instruction that begins with structured phonics lessons over instruction that omits such lessons, and even showing particular subcategories of phonics instruction to be significantly better than others. Nevertheless, the word method, redubbed "whole language," is still the dominant approach to early reading instruction in public schools. When phonics is used, it is usually cobbled onto the curriculum in an ad hoc way, rather than being part of an empirically tested and proven reading instruction curriculum.[7]

Even in mathematics, where the concept of proof is central, pedagogical methods have been chosen for their philosophical pedigrees rather than their demonstrated effectiveness. The National Council of Teachers of Mathematics recently complained that math instruction in the United States has typically not been based on sound experimental evidence, but its own curriculum guidelines are guilty of the same failing— citing the musings of philosophers rather than the evidence of successful classroom trials. Despite that fact, their unproven guidelines have been shaping mathematics instruction in many states for a decade. A 1998 study conducted by Stanford mathematics professor James Milgram found that students from one of the nation's top high schools, who were taught for four years using a curriculum closely based on the NCTM guidelines, failed to match, let alone surpass, a control group of students on any of the four achievement measures used in the study. The control group was taught using a traditional mathematics curriculum currently out of favor in most public school districts (it included Algebra I, Geometry, Algebra II, Trigonometry, and Pre-Calculus).

The preceding discussion might well leave the impression that the pedagogical error of public schooling is purely one of omission: that it has wrongly failed to empirically test instructional techniques before implementing them in classrooms. That impression would be mistaken. During the 1960s and 1970s, the federal government undertook what became a multibillion-dollar experiment called "Follow Through," comparing the effectiveness of twenty-two different pedagogical methods. Regrettably, the nation's public schools failed to follow through on this experiment, ignoring its findings and actually allowing some of the least effective methods to become the most firmly entrenched.

To this day, students in colleges of education are either taught nothing about the results of Follow Through, or they are taught the grossly misleading generalization that no one category of pedagogical methods proved consistently and significantly superior to any other. For convenience, the twenty-two participating methods had been grouped into four categories, but while the average outcomes of the four categories did not differ significantly, one individual method (Direct Instruction) actually excelled all the others.

> [Direct Instruction] not only placed first in teaching basic skills as a whole, but came out first in all four [component skills] (reading, arithmetic, spelling, and language) individually. Students taught by Direct Instruction placed a close second in advanced conceptual

skills . . . and even scored highest on tests of self-esteem and responsibility toward their work.[8]

It is truly shocking that Direct Instruction's remarkable
success has been glossed over by public schools, colleges of
education, and even leading education historians. Respected
historian Maris Vinovskis, for example, dedicates an entire
chapter to Follow Through in his recent book *History and
Educational Policymaking*, but his only reference to Direct
Instruction is a passing mention that it "may have been
somewhat more effective than other [approaches]".[9] Though
he cites the official study of Follow Through conducted by
Abt Associates, he does not report their findings on a
method-by-method basis, emphasizing instead the meaning-
less generalization that "no type of model was notably more
successful than the others."[10] As I have written elsewhere,

> In any industry subject to the demands of its customers, the clear
> superiority of a method like Direct Instruction would soon have
> displaced competing practices. Public schooling, however, is not
> one of those industries. Not only did Distar fail to catch on, many
> school systems that had used the method so successfully during
> Follow Through abandoned it shortly after the Abt study was re-
> leased. Predictably, their students' scores began to fall off. Though
> disadvantaged former Distar students continued to outperform the
> disadvantaged non-Distar control group after the program was
> terminated, their gains with respect to the national average began
> to erode as soon as they were returned to regular classrooms.[11]

U.S. public schooling's rejection of empirical testing of new
methods has contributed to a dismal record of stagnation and
decline in achievement over the past 100 years. Reading
achievement for students of a given age stagnated for the first
seventy years of the twentieth century, despite a significant increase in the length of the school year over that period.[12] Since
1970, achievement in most subjects has either continued to
stagnate or has actually declined. The rosiest trend data come
from the National Assessment of Education Progress (NAEP),
which tests representative samples of fourth, eighth, and
twelfth graders on a variety of subjects. Overall, these tests

show no significant improvement from their introduction in the late 1960s and early 1970s to the mid 1990s.[13] A grimmer picture is painted by the International Evaluation of Education Achievement (IEA), which has tested reading, mathematics, and science achievement around the world over the past three decades. A comparison of the 1970 and 1990 IEA reading tests reveals that the average score of U.S. fourteen-year-olds dropped from 602 to 541 (roughly 8 percent on the 800-point scale).[14] That was the second worst decline among the seven countries for which data were available.

Further evidence of a decline in reading achievement comes from the National Adult Literacy Survey of 1992 and the Young Adult Literacy Survey of 1985. These surveys, designed specifically to allow the measurement of changes in student performance over time, show a drop in the score of young adults from 293 to 280 on the 500-point scale.[15] The most damning verdict on American literacy has been handed down by the International Adult Literacy Survey (IALS), released in 1995. According to the IALS, one quarter of all sixteen-to-twenty-five-year-olds scored at or below the lowest level of literacy measured by the test, meaning that they would be unable to perform the sorts of reading and writing tasks required to hold, or even to apply for, most jobs.[16] That is the state of U.S. literacy after one hundred and fifty years of nearly universal government schooling.

Students' mathematics and science proficiency has not fared much better. In its First and Second International Mathematics Studies (FIMS and SIMS), the IEA tested the skills of both thirteen- and seventeen-year-olds. Between the mid 1960s and the mid 1980s, when the tests were conducted, scores for the younger students declined somewhat, while those of the older students rose. Unfortunately, the author of the study comparing the results of the two tests has indicated that the results for seventeen-year-olds are in doubt.[17]

Science scores are available for ten- and fourteen-year-olds in 1970–71 and 1983–84. IEA researchers comparing the results of these tests found that scores for U.S. ten-year-olds fell by 16 points while those of fourteen-year-olds dropped 47 points.[18] No nation suffered a worse decline over this period than the United States. In 1997, the results of the Third International Mathematics and Science Study (TIMSS) were released, but unfortunately no effort was made to allow comparisons between TIMSS results and those of earlier IEA math or science studies.

In short, while most fields of human endeavor have seen astonishing growth and improvement over the past century-and-a-half, while whole new industries have been created and general intelligence has steadily increased,[19] educational achievement alone has stagnated.

But what about Japan? Though Japanese public schools have not enjoyed the dramatic gains in effectiveness and efficiency of some other industries, their students frequently outscore their international peers academically. As it turns out, several of the most important reasons for Japan's academic success lie outside its government school system, and even though its public schools do outshine those of other countries in certain respects, they nevertheless suffer from the flaws endemic to all state-education monopolies.

Much has been written on the causes of Japan's academic success. The consensus among experts in the field points to a combination of four factors: the motivating effects of high-stakes entrance exams, cultural factors such as intense parental involvement (usually by mothers), sound pedagogy in the public schools, and perhaps most importantly, the widespread patronage of private, for-profit supplementary schools.

Because of the rigid credentialism of Japanese employers, graduates of "A-level" universities have by far the best career prospects. Acceptance by a university is, in turn, decided almost entirely as a result of written tests. The pressure to score highly on these tests is thus tremendous, and it has a trickle-down effect even on fairly early stages of formal education.

The involvement of mothers in the education of their children is also more intense in Japan than in many other nations, and it is not uncommon for mothers to take private

lessons in how to coach their children to higher performance. Schools offering such instruction are know colloquially
as *mama-juku.*

One aspect of Japanese academic success that can be directly
attributed to public schools is their generally well-chosen pedagogical approach. In comparing methods and materials used
in U.S. and Japanese schools, researchers such as Harold
Stevenson and others have noted the greater effectiveness of
Japanese instruction—particularly in mathematics and science.[20] Still, there is nothing in the public schools' procedure
for selecting pedagogical methods that will ensure the continued use of effective approaches, that will tailor existing approaches to meet changing demand, or that will spur successful
innovation and the development of new methods. For these
factors, one must look at Japan's for-profit market of after-
school schools, called *juku.*

Though they receive scant attention in the foreign press,
Japan's *juku* constitute an annual (U.S.) $5 billion private
education industry.[21] Attendance begins as early as the first
grade and becomes more and more common as children approach senior high school. By the fifth grade, one child in
three is enrolled in a *juku.* Over one half of eighth graders
were found to be enrolled in *juku* in 1991, and estimates for
ninth graders are as high as 70 percent. A Tokyo survey
found that nine out of ten students had attended a *juku* by
the time they reached the ninth grade.[22]

Within Japan, the key role *juku* play in raising the nation's
students to academic preeminence is widely recognized. The
following views are typical: "The quality of the Japanese primary and secondary educational system cannot be maintained without the support of a [supplemental] educational
system, such as *juku,* which compensates for the inflexibility
of the formal system."[23] "Without [*juku*], the success of
Japan in the area of education would be unthinkable."[24]

Where Japan's public schools offer a rigid curriculum that
leaves some children behind and others bored, *juku* tailor
their instruction to the specific needs of each child. Students

are grouped based on their performance in each subject and promoted to the next level as soon as they have mastered the material, rather than being arbitrarily promoted because of their age, as in the state system. *Juku* administer tests to determine areas where children need extra help, and target those areas with particular vigor. Though many *juku* focus on test preparation, that is only one element in an astonishingly diverse range of course offerings, including remedial and advanced academic lessons, music, swimming, and calligraphy. Fierce competition among *juku* keeps tuition costs under control, while economies of scale in the development of curricula allow larger *juku* to offer vastly higher salaries to their top teachers than is possible within any of the world's state-run education systems.

If Japan has a lesson in school governance to teach the rest of the world, it is that markets are far more responsive to the needs of the individual children they serve, and better able to cater to a wide range of demand, than the monolithic and bureaucratically calcified state monopoly.

Historical evidence on the academic effects of market versus monopoly provision is consistent with the trends observed above. Between the late 1700s and the mid 1800s, both England and the United States had steadily growing rates of literacy, and by the 1860s a significant majority of the citizens in both countries could read and write. This growth in literacy can be ascribed almost entirely to increasing public demand for basic academic skills and the ability of private and semi-public schools to meet that demand. Not only did the state play little role in fostering the spread of literacy during this period, in England it actively fought the process, fearful that the ability to read and write would lead its economic underclass to insurrection. Even after the English government eased its policies against the spread of literacy and began to provide a small education subsidy, the schools it subsidized were generally more expensive to operate than their entirely private counterparts and appear to have done an inferior job of teaching reading and writing.[25]

Reaching further back through the centuries, the civilizations regarded as having the highest literacy rates of their ages were parent-driven educational marketplaces. The ability to read and write was far more widely enjoyed in the early medieval Islamic empire and in fourth-century-B.C.E. Athens than in any other cultures of their times. In neither case did the state supply or even systematically subsidize educational services. The Muslim world's eventual introduction of state funding under Nizam al-Mulk in the eleventh century was quickly followed by partisan religious squabbling over education and the gradual fall of Islam from its place of cultural and scientific preeminence.[26]

Preparation for the workforce is another area in which state schooling has failed to show itself superior to competitive educational markets. The U.S. business community has so little confidence in the value of a high school education that grades and other school factors are given less consideration in hiring decisions than any other qualifications. Candidates' previous work experience, general disposition, and communication skills are all given more weight.[27] This skepticism is amply justified, given the dismal statistics regarding the skills of entry-level job candidates and the increasing need for businesses to teach their new employees basic academic skills. Though 90 percent of high school seniors polled in 1997 believed themselves prepared for immediate entry into the workforce, only half of all employers agreed. While 92 percent of the seniors thought their written communication skills were sufficient for the workplace, only 45 percent of employers concurred with that assessment.[28] *Training* magazine reports that while 18 percent of American businesses provided basic remedial instruction for their employees in 1984, the figure had leapt to 43 percent by 1995.[29] Across the country, one-third of American businesses report that their employees' poor learning skills are preventing them from reorganizing work responsibilities.[30]

While the United States currently lacks a competitive educational market against which to compare these poor public schooling results, the historical evidence suggests independent and competing schools have had more success in conveying practical employment skills than contemporary government systems. In the wake of the Reformation, for example, Martin Luther and his friend Melanchthon entreated the leaders of the German states to introduce state schools that would produce classically trained graduates fluent in Latin. That goal did not generally coincide with the will of the common people, who sought more career-oriented training for their children. The municipality of Heidenheim was a fairly typical case, in which merchants and community leaders objected when their local German school was summarily closed and replaced with a tax-supported Latin one. In a letter to their Duke, they wrote: "Our young people, most of whom have no aptitude for Latin and are growing up to be artisans, are better served by a German teacher than a Latin master, for they need to learn writing and reading, which is of great help to them in their work and livelihood."[31]

It would be incorrect, however, to jump to the conclusion that private ownership is a guarantee that schools will more effectively meet parents' demands for career preparation. The privately endowed grammar schools of eighteenth- and nineteenth-century England are a case in point. Because these schools were funded predominantly or wholly by wealthy benefactors rather than through fees, they tended to teach the things that the donors stipulated, regardless of the demands of families. Since the donors were very often landed gentry who had themselves received a classical Latin education devoid of science, modern languages, and job training, they insisted on the same for students of the schools they endowed.

Parents would have none of it. Enrollment in endowed grammar schools dropped steadily from the late 1700s onward, as new fee-charging independent schools sprang up to offer lessons more in keeping with parents' demands.

> Subjects long ignored by the grammar schools began to appear, and soon entirely new ones were added. Arithmetic and geography were among the first, and these were joined by anatomy, biology,

bookkeeping, economics, surveying, naval studies, and many others. While sometimes maintaining vestiges of the traditional curriculum, private institutions usually allotted them less time and importance than the new subjects. . . . In keeping with the applied scientific nature of many of the [new] courses, experiments using telescopes, microscopes and other devices complemented familiar teaching methods.[32]

Even as far back as classical Athens, apprenticeships were practiced alongside formal schooling, ensuring that students would have a marketable skill by the end of their education. This combination of academic instruction and practical training helped to make Athens the economic superpower of its time. By the fourth century B.C.E., Athens' booming economy could boast joint-stock corporations and a thriving insurance industry many centuries before these became common in the rest of the world. The public school system of ancient Sparta, focusing as it did solely on military training, taught no career skills at all and thus stunted the city-state's economic development.

Today, career-focused higher education is one of the fastest-growing sectors of the education industry, with institutions such as the for-profit University of Phoenix opening branch campuses all over the United States, demonstrating an ability to meet growing demand that far exceeds the norm among public and non-profit private universities.

SERVING DIVERSE COMMUNITIES AND FOSTERING SOCIAL HARMONY

As noted in the Introduction, there are areas of both consensus and of disagreement among parents regarding the things they want their children to learn. Though academic training and career preparation garner nearly universal support, there are wide disparities in areas such as the teaching of history and social studies, sex education, and religion. Even people of the same faith sometimes disagree about the role of religion in schooling, with some feeling that the two can, or should, be kept separate, and others believing that they must be fully integrated.

Fortunately, these differences of opinion need not lead to conflict. Though it is common for people to wish that others would share their views on controversial issues, few people actually want to compel their fellow citizens to adopt their own values through the force of law. Consider the public school prayer issue in the United States. A majority of U.S. citizens favor prayer at their local schools—unless some parents strongly object. In cases where there are objections, support for school prayer drops to a minority.[33] For an educational system to serve the public's aims, therefore, it must be able to cater to a wide range of demands without forcing the views of one group on any other.

Public schooling has not done a good job of fulfilling that goal, either in modern times or historically. On issues ranging from the founding of our nation to the origin of our species, public schools have tended to formally entrench one view at the expense of others. In 1992, for example, Florida enacted a statute requiring that public school children be made to "understand that a specific culture is not intrinsically superior or inferior to another." This was not a self-evident principle with which all the state's residents agreed. In fact, it was so contrary to the views of some Floridian parents that the Lake County School Board passed its own requirement that the public schools teach "our republican form of government, capitalism, a free enterprise system, patriotism, strong family values, freedom of religion, and other basic values that are superior to other foreign or historic cultures." Whatever one's views on the relative merits of the two positions, it is clear that they were at odds with one another. In the end, the courts upheld the state's power to impose its will on the public schools, regardless of the dissent voiced by local communities.

The most pervasive and intractable case of public schools failing to serve the demands of all families is their inability to offer devotional religious instruction. This is extraordinarily frustrating to parents who wish to provide their children with a thoroughly religious educational environment, particularly because those parents are obliged to pay for the very schools that cannot cater to their needs. Many orthodox Protestant families also have beliefs about the origins of man that conflict with the scientific consensus on evolution. Contrary to these parents' wishes, the public schools have not, and in fact cannot, pass their beliefs on to their children. To minimize the offense given to orthodox Protestant families, many public school districts have watered down their presentation of the theory of evolution, in some cases omitting it entirely.[34] Not only has this failed to fully satisfy believers in the Biblical creation story, it has angered parents who wish to see the theory of evolution presented with depth and clarity. No group has been well-served on the issue.

Ironically, the modern problem of public schooling's inability to deliver devotional religious instruction is a reversal of the problem that existed prior to the mid twentieth century, when Protestant religious activities were common in public schools. Irish Catholics were singled out for attack by early public schools, with one nineteenth-century textbook claiming that America was becoming "the common sewer of Ireland." The New York City school board did offer at one point to "remove any particular instances of religious slander from its textbooks that the Catholic Bishop cared to list, but there was no question of removing the Protest Bible altogether," or of letting Catholics use their own Bible in the public schools. It was not uncommon for Catholic children to be whipped or beaten for refusing to read from the Protestant Bible, and the Supreme Courts of several states upheld the right of school districts to do so.[35]

The inability of U.S. state-run schools to serve the moral and religious educational demands of its diverse population is not an aberration. The same has been true of governmental school systems throughout history. In post-revolutionary France, Protestant republicans and Catholic royalists treaded equally heavily on the prerogatives of families, alternately foisting the Catholic Bible on students and tearing it from their hands. In the early sixteenth century, the German state schools championed by Luther and his fellow reformers trampled the people's growing interest in practical studies, imposing instead a classical Latin program (particularly at the secondary level of education). In the Islamic empire of the eleventh century, the introduction of state education funding and subsequent state control over schools greatly curtailed the freedom of families to obtain the kind of education they wanted for their children. The list of similar cases is long.[36]

The record of independent schools in serving the needs of diverse communities is considerably better. Competitive markets have tended to offer a broader range of educational options to parents, and have done a superior job of identifying changes in demand over time. In contrast to the homogeneous and homogenizing public schools of classical Sparta, the free educational market of Athens embraced a vastly wider range of subjects and treated them from a variety of different viewpoints. Parents and their children were free to choose from among the available options as they saw fit. The same was true in the early part of the medieval Muslim empire (from the eighth through the eleventh century).

Today, independent schools cater to people of many different faiths, from Catholics and Jews to Protestants and Muslims. Curricula focus on the arts or the sciences, on international languages and cultures, or on the history and traditions of particular groups. All this diversity, which clearly exceeds that found within the government sector, has been achieved despite the fact that independent schools enroll roughly one-tenth as many students as the state schools.

Few advocates of state schooling have seriously argued that government schools are better able to cater to a diverse clientele. More commonly, they argue that it is precisely the market's ability to cater to diversity that makes it dangerous. They fear that if parents could really get what they want for their children, it would balkanize our society into warring factions. This apprehension is not only unsupported by the evidence, it is exactly backward.

It is not the patrons of private Atheist Academies and Evangelical Elementaries who tear into one another on the subject of evolution versus creation. It is not the private Afrocentric school, or Orthodox Jewish school, or Classical Western Culture school that sows dissension among the families in its neighborhood. It was not the private Catholic primary school of nineteenth-century America that drove its community into a frenzy by foisting its version of the Bible on all the local children. It was, however, the state schools of post-revolutionary France that set citizen against citizen by favoring republican or royalist views according to the whim of despots; and it is the modern U.S. public school system that factionalizes the population on issues of curriculum and religion, eating away at the fabric of the nation year after year like the relentless action of waves eroding what could be a peaceful shore.[37]

The reason why state school systems have produced so much more confrontation than educational markets is that compulsion, not diversity, is the chief culprit in creating educational conflict. When parents have been able to obtain the particular educational services they have wanted for their children without having to force their preferences on their neighbors, frustrations and antagonisms have been kept to a minimum. Apart from the exceptional trial of Socrates, the classical Athenian education market was not a source of conflict. The only notable competition was between teachers, as they tried to enroll new students by arguing that their own knowledge and methods were superior to those of their competitors.

One of the most dramatic examples of how education markets have permitted the peaceful coexistence of disparate groups is the case of early medieval Islam. Skeptics and agnostics coexisted with orthodox Muslims, and both in turn were generally tolerant of Hebrews and Christians. Historian Abraham Blinderman observes that: "Perhaps few other periods in the tragic history of the Jewish people have been as meaningful to them as this period of Judaeo-Arabic communion. The renaissance of Jewish letters and science in Arab lands is a glorious testimonial to the cultural cosmopolitanism of the Arabs at a time when Jews in Europe were being burned as witches, plague-begetters, and ritualistic murderers."[38]

In the eleventh century, however, state funding and control of education was introduced to the Muslim world, and the tolerance that had been enjoyed under the educational marketplace was lost. Not only were different religions thrown into conflict by the government schools, but the two principal branches of Islam were turned against one another as well.

We are all losers when our differing views become declarations of war; when, instead of allowing many distinct communities of ideas to coexist harmoniously, our schools force us to battle one another in a needless and destructive fight for ideological supremacy. If U.S. churches were run by the state as schools have been, we would have had as many religious wars in this nation as we have had school wars. We can learn a lesson from the peaceful coexistence of our private mosques, cathedrals, synagogues, and shrines: it is possible to celebrate both our varied traditions and the common ideals on which our nation is based. The totalitarian notion that schools should sanction one set of views at the expense of all others is surely not among those American ideals.

A SAFE AND STUDIOUS ENVIRONMENT

"School Crime Is Declining,"[39] assures a recent booklet published by the Center on Education Policy. The Center, and many other public school advocacy groups, base this assurance on a statistic included in the government publication *Indicators of School Crime and Safety 1999*.[40] That statistic is the percentage of students who were criminally victimized at school during the previous six months, and it declined from 15.5 percent in 1993 to 10.2 percent in 1997. There are several serious problems with this statistic and with the broad implications that are imputed to it. Before addressing the problems with the statistic itself, however, it is worth mentioning that the original table in the *Indicators* study reports data for years 1992 through 1997 and that the crime rate reported for 1992 (14.4 percent) was lower than that for 1993.[41] The Center on Education Policy's decision to choose the higher 1993 figure as its initial benchmark instead of the lower 1992 figure is left curiously unexplained.

More importantly, the statistic in question only includes students from twelve to eighteen years of age (excluding older high school seniors), and it fails to disaggregate the data for public versus private school students. As it happens, the *Indicators of School Crime and Safety 1999* study provides other statistics that do distinguish between public and private schools and that include students from twelve to nineteen years old. The period covered is also somewhat broader, reaching from 1989 to 1995. Over that time span, the percentage of public school students reporting criminal victimization rose slightly from 14.7 to 14.8 percent, whereas the figure for private school students fell from 12.8 percent to 12.4 percent.[42] Public school crime thus does not appear to have declined since the 1980s, although private school crime does. The absolute crime rate is also lower in private than in public schools.

This picture is repeated in numerous other statistics included in the *Indicators* study. Public school students, for example, are twice as likely to be violently assaulted as private school students, are four-and-a-half times as likely to report gang activity at school,[43] and are four times more likely to avoid certain places at school out of fear.[44] These differences, moreover, exist whether the public and private schools in question are rural, suburban, or urban. In central city schools, the differences between the public and private sector are generally as large as, or even larger than, those just described. Even teachers cannot escape these differences, with public school teachers being twice as likely as private school teachers to report having been physically attacked or threatened with injury in the past twelve months.

In many cases these situations are worsening over time. Between 1989 and 1995, the percentage of students reporting gang activity in public schools nearly doubled from 16.5 percent to 30.6 percent. Such reports also increased in the private sector, but far more modestly: from 4.4 percent to

6.8 percent. In 1995 and 1997, "almost one-third of all students in grades 9 through 12 . . . reported that someone had offered, sold, or given them an illegal drug on school property,"[45] a significant increase from the 24 percent figure reported in 1993. A poll of teachers reveals how different the public and independent school environments are:

> The private sector suffers only one-fifth the rate of student absenteeism, half the rate of teacher absenteeism, and one-sixth the rate of physical conflicts between students as the public sector. Vandalism, crime, drug abuse, student disrespect for teachers, all are vastly lower among independent schools. Student apathy, viewed as a serious problem by a fifth of all public school teachers, concerns only one out of every twenty-five private school teachers. . . . Critics would claim that these advantages result [entirely] from the kinds of families who opt for independent schooling, rather than from the schools themselves. . . . They would be wrong. An extensive study of Catholic independent schools has revealed that even adjusting for a host of socioeconomic and demographic factors, [independent] schools exert a significant positive effect on the behavior and morale of both students and teachers.[46]

AFFORDABILITY AND EFFICIENCY

Parents and the public at large have only so much income they are willing and able to spend on education, and so both affordability and efficiency are prime goals. It is important to note, therefore, that one of the chief arguments made by public schooling's nineteenth-century advocates was that the large centralized system they proposed would be more efficient than the seemingly disorganized market of small schools that existed at the time. In keeping with their proposed strategy, schools and districts have been getting bigger for more than a century. Between 1929–30 and 1993–1994, the number of one-room schoolhouses fell from roughly 150,000 to 442. Today, the majority of public high school children attend institutions enrolling over a thousand students. In 1932, after years of consolidation, there were still 127,531 school districts nationwide. By 1962, the number had dropped to 35,676, and it has continued to decline until, in the 1993–1994 school year, only 14,881 districts remained.

This relentless process of centralization has not produced the windfall in efficiency that was promised. At roughly $7,000 per student, annual public school expenditures are now more than double the average tuition charged by private schools. Even after taking into account parish subsidies and other sources of funding available to religious schools, the government sector still spends vastly more per student than its private counterpart. Moreover, public schools spent fourteen times as much per pupil in 1996 as they did in 1920, after adjusting for inflation.

These dismal national statistics are echoed at the level of individual schools and districts. During the 1980s, several investigators analyzed the effect of public school spending on student achievement by surveying the results of many small-scale studies. The best known of these investigators was economist Eric Hanushek, who found that there was generally no significant relationship between spending and achievement. He concluded, in other words, that higher per-pupil spending in the public school system usually had little effect on student performance.

Hanushek's findings were roundly attacked, and both his raw data and his conclusions were called into question. One of the most frequently heard criticisms was that the studies Hanushek analyzed were of varying quality and that some were out of date, coming from as far back as the 1920s. This criticism was addressed, however, in a separate investigation conducted by professors Stephen Childs and Charol Shakeshaft. With some disappointment, Childs and Shakeshaft also conceded that "the relationship between student achievement and level of educational expenditures is minimal." Furthermore, they found that public schools have actually been getting less efficient over time. The older studies for which Hanushek had been criticized actually showed greater public school efficiency than the more recent ones.

Other research has led to similarly disappointing conclusions, such as the fact that large public schools and districts make worse, not better, use of their resources than the smaller institutions they supplanted. We should not be surprised by these findings when the public school systems of major metropolitan areas employ five, ten, or even fifty times as many central administrators per student as the private Catholic school systems in those same metropolitan areas. Worse yet, large schools tend to introduce many negative side-effects along the way. Professor Alan Ornstein's one-sentence summary of the literature is particularly damning: "Current consensus correlates small schools with school effectiveness, community and school identity, and individual fulfillment and participation, and large schools with school inefficiency, institutional bureaucracy, and personal loneliness."

The history of free educational markets exhibits a different trend. As mentioned in the section on academic achievement, the state-subsidized schools of nineteenth-century England appear to have been both more expensive to operate and less effective at spreading literacy than their entirely independent, fee-charging competitors. Though cost comparisons are difficult when we go further back in history, it seems clear that a vigorous competition among schools kept tuition fees low in the educational market of classical Athens. That same effect can be found today in the Japanese market for the for-profit after-school schools known as *juku*. Competition among *juku* has kept prices sufficiently low, so that 90 percent of children attend these schools for some period of time.

Market education's higher efficiency does not necessarily translate into greater affordability for all parents, however. Though independent schools can generally educate students for much less than their public sector counterparts with equal or better results, parents do not pay tuition directly to public schools. Poor families can thus avail themselves of a system that will spend roughly $84,000 on twelve years of schooling for each of their children, but they may not be able to spend more than a small fraction of that amount out of their own pockets. Since one of the public's most deeply and widely held goals is to ensure that all children have access to a good education regardless of income, this is a serious dilemma, and it is taken up again below.

SERVING THE DISADVANTAGED

One of Horace Mann's noblest promises was that the public schools would do an excellent job of serving the needs of the disadvantaged. It is a promise that public schools have not been able to keep. Though most inner city districts serving poor populations spend six to ten thousand dollars per pupil every year, they have proven themselves incapable of such basic tasks as providing stall doors and toilet paper for their bathrooms. They have often neglected even the most routine maintenance of plumbing, heating, and roofing systems, resulting in costly damage to school buildings and the demoralization of both students and teachers. Metal detectors, drug-sniffing dogs, and armed police have become commonplace. These schools have lost their ability to provide a safe and studious environment for many urban children.[47]

While racial integration has been a stated goal of U.S. public schools for forty years, those schools are little more integrated today than they were before the first mandatory busing plan was introduced. Independent schools, by contrast, have become vastly more integrated during the past four decades, and, according to recent research, now offer a more genuinely integrated environment than do public schools.

In the 1968–69 school year, 93 percent of all independent school students were non-Hispanic whites, 3.6 percent African-Americans, and 3.3 percent of other racial or ethnic groups. Thirty years later, the percentage of African-Americans in independent schools has almost tripled to 9.1 percent, approaching the (12.6 percent) proportion of African-Americans in the population at large. The overall percentage of minority students in independent schools has leapt from 6.9 percent to 22 percent during the same period. Even after this rapid rise, the rate of growth in black independent school enrollment continues to outpace that of total independent school enrollment or white independent school enrollment.[48]

Far more minority children are now attending independent schools than was previously the case, but how well integrated are those schools? To find out, Sociologist James Coleman compared integration figures[49] for public schools, Catholic schools, and non-Catholic private schools during the 1980s. Of the three sectors, non-Catholic independent schools had the least African-American/white segregation, followed by the Catholic schools. Coleman found public schools to be the most segregated—a stunning finding given that public school systems across the country were under legal orders to integrate their student populations.[50]

But how much do students of different racial and ethnic backgrounds really interact with one another even when they attend the same schools? Does the level of such interaction differ between the public and private sectors? Professor Jay Greene and his colleague Nicole Mellow cleverly addressed that question in 1998, by observing the voluntary seating choices of students in school lunchrooms. This, they reasoned, was a far more meaningful measure of integration than overall district or even school-level enrollment figures. What they found is that students in private (particularly religious) schools were much more likely to choose lunch partners of other races than were students in public schools.[51]

Advocates for state schooling often counter such evidence by referring back to the ideal that public schools must accept all comers, while independent schools can pick and chose their students, and may simply refuse to serve some children. Whatever the ideal of state schooling, the reality is quite different. The public schools in just twenty-two states send 100,000 of their most difficult-to-educate students to the private sector, according to a recent study by the Mackinac Center in Michigan.[52] The Washington D.C. public school district alone sends more than a thousand special education students to private schools every year because it is unable to serve those students.[53]

There is no dispute that the quality of education provided by central city districts is generally inferior to that provided by their suburban counterparts. In fact, the evidence shows that economic and racial achievement gaps are larger within the public school system than they are within the private sector. Poor inner city children who attend private Catholic schools do better academically and are far more likely to graduate from high school and to go on to college than public school students from similar backgrounds, and racial and economic achievement gaps are smaller in Catholic schools than in government schools.[54]

This evidence flies in the face of the widespread belief that children from low-income families would be left uneducated if it were not for the existence of fully tax-funded government schools. As history shows, poor parents not only saw to their children's education before the state intervened, they often chose to assume the financial burden of private fee-charging schools because they preferred the services of those schools to the offerings of state-subsidized institutions. In mid-nineteenth-century England, one key difference between the two sorts of institutions was that teachers in subsidized schools were appointed by the school operators, not selected by parents. Because the people running subsidized schools rarely had children attending them, there was little personal incentive for them to ensure the teachers' competency. Sometimes sound selections were made, but in the worst cases, instructors were appointed who would never have been able to draw paying students. It was also not uncommon for schools subsidized by the government and/or by religious societies to omit the teaching of writing, on the grounds that "Reading will help to mend people's morals, but writing is not necessary [for the lower classes]."[55] Fee-charging private-venture schools, by contrast, taught whatever parents paid them to teach. As a result, the appeal of subsidized schools was limited. "The subsidized, endowed and charity schools of Manchester attracted only 8 percent of all those attending schools and there were empty places available."[56] It took many decades and a significant increase in education taxes and state education spending before the majority of low-income families were lured away from their private-venture schools.

This, however, brings us back to the problem outlined earlier: while low-income families generally receive better quality services from competitive markets than from state monopolies, they cannot necessarily afford to purchase the quantity of services that they and the public believe their children should enjoy. A proposed solution to this problem is described in the section titled Understanding Excellence.

FOSTERING PARENTAL INVOLVEMENT AND RESPONSIBILITY

The importance of ensuring that parents are actively involved in their children's education is universally recognized. What is not so widely known is that the very nature of government-run, tax-funded schooling discourages that involvement. Before the introduction of state schooling, parents were obliged to make all the major decisions regarding their children's education: where they would go to school, who would teach them, what they would study, for how long they would attend, and how much that schooling was worth. Over the years, the state school system has usurped the right to make virtually all of those decisions, leaving to parents little more than the task of waking their children in the morning and pointing them toward the school bus. By wresting away parents' rights and responsibilities, public schools have consigned them to the role of spectators in their own children's education. Parents who do try to take an active role are so often ignored or rebuffed that frustration and eventual surrender are the all-too-frequent outcomes. When parents held the educational purse strings, they held the reins of educational power. Today, the schools have a new and fickle master—a vast bureaucratic empire putatively accountable to everyone but in reality accountable to no one.

The need for parental financial responsibility is not a new insight. Consider the case of a successful lawyer born in the early sixties. After discovering that the small town where he grew up was still without its own high school, he decided to found one himself—but, though he could have fully endowed the school, he chose to pay only one-third of the necessary costs. He explained this decision in a letter to a friend, writing that he had seen grave problems wherever teachers' salaries were paid from public funds and that parents could be encouraged to choose teachers wisely through their obligation to contribute to the cost of the school. That lawyer's name was Pliny the Younger. He was a citizen of the Roman Empire, born in the early sixties of the first century C.E.

During the mid nineteenth century, as fully tax-funded schooling was taking hold in the United States, Canada, and elsewhere, a few prophetic individuals once again voiced the need for direct financial responsibility for parents. In 1847, the Honorable Robert Spence of Canada "was certain that the granting of free schools would undermine parental responsibility in educational matters. Once the parent ceased to pay for the schooling of his children, the crucial link between himself and the teachers was severed, and a gradual decline in family interest in the schools would take place."[57]

The truth of Pliny's and Spence's observations can still be seen today in the differences between tuition-charging schools and tax-funded schools. According to U.S. Department of Education statistics, public school teachers are seven times more likely to complain about parent apathy than private school teachers. While the problem has been getting worse over time in public schools, it has been improving in private ones,[58] and this difference is not a symptom of self-selection. When a random sample of poor Milwaukee parents received private school vouchers, their involvement in their children's education increased significantly with respect to that of a control group that did not receive vouchers and had to remain in the public schools.

Parents are so often apathetic toward government schools because they have little meaningful power or responsibility over them. When asked how much control they felt parents had over six different aspects of their children's public school education, a significant majority of Gallup poll respondents said "very little" or "almost none" on every issue from curriculum and textbooks to teacher selection and salaries. As any parent knows, responsibilities breed responsibility. Unless parents have the power to make the important decisions regarding their children's education, they will inevitably become marginalized. Historically, the only way that parents consistently retained that power was by directly paying for their children's education.

EDUCATION FOR, AND ABOUT, DEMOCRACY

Most citizens want their schools to not only prepare children for successful private lives, but also to equip them for their duties as citizens. By this measure, public schooling is falling short of expectations. During the 1980s, philosopher and constitutional scholar Mortimer Adler conducted innumerable high school discussions on the key political texts of the United States. In discussing the Declaration of Independence, he was dismayed to find that, almost without exception, students had never before read that document. Time and again he found that high school students did not understand the meaning of the Declaration's principal terms and that their lack of understanding extended to the Constitution and Gettysburg Address. He concluded that the students' grasp of these documents failed to approach even the minimum level required for intelligent citizenship.

Adler's findings are sadly consistent with those of the U.S. history portion of the National Assessment of Educational Progress. Results on these nationwide tests are expected to fall into one of three score ranges: basic, proficient, or advanced. Remarkably, the majority of high school seniors actually scored below the lowest ("basic") level in 1994 (the most recent year for which test results are available). Their grasp of this nation's history was so poor as to place them off the charts. Is the achievement standard set too high? When asked in 1988 to identify the half-century during which the Constitution was drafted, 40 percent of high school seniors answered incorrectly. Two-thirds did not know that the Civil War took place during the second half of the nineteenth century. Only two students in five could correctly identify the purpose of *The Federalist* papers, and one out of every three students did not know that the Declaration of Independence marked the formal severance of the colonies from Britain.

Based on a recent nationwide study of Latino Americans, it appears that nongovernmental schools do a better job than governmental schools of promoting participation in civic life, even after adjusting for differences in student socioeconomic status and the educational background of their parents. Latinos educated in independent schools are more likely to vote, are more tolerant of other groups, and participate more often in charitable, social, and business organizations, than Latinos educated in public schools.[59] Certainly the independent Catholic schools attended by much of the Kennedy family, and the home-schooling and private tutoring received by Franklin Delano Roosevelt, do not appear to have impeded their interest or success in public service.

UNDERSTANDING EXCELLENCE

There is certainly considerable variation in outcomes among the education systems discussed above. Some of that variation can be explained by differences in culture, by economic factors, or simply by chance. But when we apply the three-pronged analysis described in the Introduction to this paper, a trend does emerge: markets of independent and competing schools generally do a better job of meeting the public's needs than uncompetitive state-run systems.

While it is true, for example, that the modern Japanese public school system is more effective in some areas than U.S. public schooling, such differences pale in comparison to the consistent historical superiority of market over monopoly provision. Even today, to continue with the same example,

much of Japan's success on international tests can be attributed to its vast and dynamic market of for-profit *juku* schools.

But what is responsible for the greater effectiveness of education markets? A tentative answer to that question can be
found by looking at the strengths and weaknesses of the several market-based educational systems we have explored.
My own conclusion is that the following five factors are the
necessary and sufficient ingredients for a viable educational
market:

- parental choice
- direct financial responsibility for parents
- freedom for educators
- competition between schools
- the profit motive for schools

Over the centuries, the choices made by parents in the educational marketplace have been consistently better than
those imposed upon them by government-appointed experts.
Parents have by no means been perfect, but they have usually steered away from pedagogical fads and have focused on
more useful skills. The societies and economies that have
grown up around parent-driven educational markets have
been among the most productive and cohesive in history.

Parental choice, however, is not distributed to any and all
who ask for it. It has to be fought for, and defended, as with
all other human freedoms. Schools that have not charged tuition have typically not taken the needs of families as their
guiding principle. Many have ignored those needs completely,
preferring to deliver the sort of education favored by those
who were footing the bill. Parents who try to take an active
role in schools for which they are not paying tuition are often
rebuffed as nuisances, because they have no direct power
over the institution and frequently have few alternatives.

Worse yet, "free" government schools tend eventually to
be taken for granted by parents who have many other im-

portant concerns to attend to. Government schooling whispers a dangerous siren song: "We're experts," it says. "We have your children's education well in hand." Burdened by so many other responsibilities, parents want to believe these overweening promises and gradually find themselves disenfranchised spectators to their own children's education.

Public school teachers cite the lack of participation by parents as one of their most pressing problems, but public schooling itself is one of the key causes of that problem. Private school teachers report parent apathy to be far less common. The responsibility of directly paying all or part of their children's tuition forces parents to take a more active role and gives them considerably more power over the content and direction of the instruction their children receive. Difficulties of course arise in the case of very poor families, and I'll return to those difficulties in a moment.

Just as parents need to be free to choose their children's schools, educators need to be free to innovate. They must be able to cater to specific audiences, to leverage their particular talents, and to pursue missions and philosophies of their own choosing. The absence of these freedoms leads to frustration and low morale among teachers, to inefficiency, and to pedagogical stagnation.

The freedom of schools needs to be balanced, however, to prevent abuses. Schools that are not directly answerable to families can, and do, go off on their own educational tangents that diverge wildly from the goals of the students and parents. The way to ensure that schools are free to do whatever they want so long as they are effectively serving their customers is to force them to compete with one another to attract and keep those customers.

By themselves, the four factors thus far described (choice and financial responsibility for parents, and freedom and competition for schools) are enough to prevent the worst educational abuses, but they are not enough to promote educational excellence on a long-term, widespread basis. For that, it is necessary to introduce the incentive of profit making. The absence of the profit motive in any business leads to stagnation, and the nonprofit private school industry is a case in point. The virtual absence of significant progress in pedagogy and educational technology over the past one hundred years is absolutely unprecedented in other fields, and even the best nonprofit private schools have failed to substantially expand their enrollments over the past century. Every other area of human endeavor, from agriculture to the service sector to athletics, has registered significant gains during the twentieth century—gains that have been conspicuously absent from both public and nonprofit private schools. The only proven way of spurring that same tremendous progress in education is by encouraging innovation through the lure of potential profits.

But what about low-income families? How can we ensure that they are fully able to participate in the education marketplace? For the past few years, the most common answer to that question has been government funded vouchers. When viewed in the context of the preceding discussion, however, the following serious problems emerge:

1. Vouchers for the full cost of a child's education eliminate direct parental financial responsibility, greatly increasing the likelihood that parents will lose control over their children's education and eventually become disenfranchised.

2. By separating payment from consumption, vouchers create an incentive structure conducive to fraud, corruption, and mismanagement.

3. Under a single-payer voucher system, the main avenue for schools to increase their incomes would be to lobby the state, rather than to improve the services they offer to families.

4. Universal government funding of all schools, including formerly independent schools, would spread the suffocating pall of regulation over the entire education industry, as a host of special interest groups lobbied to control the sort of education that voucher-redeeming schools could legally deliver.

5. Government vouchers leave open the possibility that citizens would be obliged by the force of law to pay for the support of religious institutions. Whether or not such a voucher program were found to be constitutional, this would be a serious problem in a free society.

It would be possible to design a government program that would somewhat abate these problems, but even if that were done, there would be little to prevent that program from being degraded by subsequent legislatures.

Fortunately, there is an alternative: finance scholarships privately and provide them on the basis of need. Those families who, without the current heavy burden of education taxes, could afford to educate their own children would do so, whereas their less financially well-off fellow citizens would receive nongovernmental subsidies. These subsidies, moreover, could be allocated on a sliding scale, ensuring that families who could afford to pay for at least part of their children's education were encouraged to do so, thereby promoting their interest and involvement in that education.

There are already roughly forty private K–12 scholarship programs in the United States. Government is not involved in any way, and the satisfaction ratings of participating families are as high as, or higher than, any other group of parents with school-aged children.[60] Currently, because public schools are still thought of as the official providers of education, these private scholarship-granting agencies raise relatively small amounts of money and educate only a few hundred or a few thousand students each. This need not be the case. If the public becomes convinced of the superiority of private scholarships in competitive markets over state-schooling monopolies, and especially if they are encouraged to donate to these philanthropic programs through tax credits, private scholarships could provide a practical and efficient system for subsidizing the education of all low-income families. Arizona already has a very small tax credit for those who donate to private scholarship programs, the

Michigan-based Mackinac Center has drafted a proposal for a much more potent law, and a pair of promising education-tax-credit proposals is currently being floated in New Jersey.

Parents have already registered their own views on private scholarship programs: when the Children's Scholarship Fund held a lottery to distribute 40,000 scholarships to low-income families in 1999, it received one-and-a-quarter million applications. Even more remarkably, the means-tested CSF scholarships required a co-payment of roughly $1,000 from participants, to ensure that they would have a vested interest in their children's schools and education. Given the income cut-off for program participants, this co-payment represents a significant financial sacrifice.

A more comprehensive discussion of the risks associated with government voucher programs and the private scholarship alternative can be found in *Market Education: The Unknown History*. The discussion of these issues in professor James Tooley's recent book *Reclaiming Education* is also very highly recommended.

CONCLUSION: IDEALS OVER INSTITUTIONS

The U.S. Declaration of Independence proclaims that governments are instituted by and among the people to secure certain fundamental ends and that "whenever any Form of Government becomes destructive of these Ends, it is the Right of the People to alter or to abolish it, and to institute new Government, laying its Foundation on such Principles, and organizing its Powers in such Form, as to them shall seem most likely to effect their Safety and Happiness."

These principles remain true today and apply to individual institutions as well as to entire governments. State-run schooling was instituted in this nation to fulfill the public's educational goals and ideals. It has not only fallen short of that aim, but has in fact run counter to it in many respects. After one-hundred-and-fifty years of trying vainly to make state schooling live up to our personal expectations and our shared ideals, is it not time we considered alternatives?

NOTES

1. Andrew J. Coulson, *Market Education: The Unknown History* (New Brunswick, N.J.: Transaction, 1999), Chapter 1.
2. In economically undeveloped societies, each family is generally forced to provide for most of its own basic needs. The division of labor and the specialization it allows are thus rare, leading to inefficient production. Because of this inefficiency, most people (including children) are forced to spend the bulk of their days working, having little time or resources left over for other pursuits. Under such circumstances, mass demand for formal education is nonexistent. It is only after economies are sufficiently advanced to allow considerable leisure time for children, and enjoy greater efficiency and the division of labor, that the population at large can and does demand organized schooling. Because of this reality, the present study is concerned only with societies that have passed the aforementioned economic threshold.

   A corollary of the previous observation is that the absence of a state-run school system does not imply the existence of a free education market. The European "Dark Ages" had neither educational markets nor state-run educational systems for the masses. Indeed, state-run schooling for the general public has rarely appeared, except where education markets were already well established. For a description of the process by which education markets generally arise, see Andrew J. Coulson, "Can Markets Work?" a paper presented to the Harvard Conference On Rethinking School Governance, Kennedy School of Government, Harvard University, June 13, 1997.
3. Nila B. Smith, *American Reading Instruction: Its Development and Its Significance in Gaining a Perspective on Current Practices in Reading* (New York: Silver, Burdett, 1934): 222.
4. Herbert M. Kliebard, *The Struggle for the American Curriculum* (New York: Routledge, 1995): 41.
5. Mitford Mathews, *Teaching to Read, Historically Considered* (Chicago: University of Chicago Press, 1966): 136.
6. Charlemagne tried desperately to learn to read and write, by some accounts sleeping with a writing tablet under his pillow, so that he could practice in his few free moments.
7. Coulson, *Market Education, op. cit.,* 160–68.
8. Coulson, *op. cit.,* 154–57.

9. Maris A. Vinovskis, *History and Educational Policymaking* (New Haven: Yale University Press, 1999): 112.

10. Vinovskis, 98. Emphasis added.

11. Coulson, *Market Education*, 154–57. And Engelmann 1992, 5–6.

12. Coulson, *Market Education*, 178. See also Lawrence C. Stedman and Carl F. Kaestle, "Literacy and Reading Performance in the United States from 1880 to the Present," in *Literacy in the United States: Readers and Reading Since 1880* (New Haven: Yale University Press, 1991): 127.

13. Coulson, *Market Education*, 179–81.

14. Petra Lietz, *Changes in Reading Comprehension Across Cultures and Over Time* (Münster: Waxmann, 1996).

15. I. S. Kirsch, L. Jenkins, A. Jungeblut, and A. Kolstad, *Adult Literacy in America* (Washington, D.C.: National Center for Education Statistics, U.S. Department of Education, 1993). Though the racial and/or ethnic composition of the test-taking population changed somewhat in the intervening years, a breakdown of the data shows that both white and Hispanic scores suffered real declines on all three subtests although the scores of blacks were mixed. White scores declined by 9 points on all three subtests. Hispanic scores declined by 20, 10, and 14 points, respectively. And scores for blacks rose by 8 points and 6 points, on the first two tests, respectively, although dropping by 7 points on the last test. The racial and /or ethnic breakdown was 76 percent white, 7 percent Hispanic, and 13 percent black in 1985, and 70 percent white, 15 percent Hispanic, and 11 percent black in 1992. No other racial and/or ethnic breakdowns were provided.

16. Organization for Economic Cooperation and Development & Statistics Canada, *Literacy, Economy and Society* (Paris: OECD, 1995): 152–54.

17. David F. Robitaille, "Achievement Comparisons between the First and Second IEA Studies of Mathematics," *Educational Studies in Mathematics* 21 (1990): 395–414.

18. John P. Keeves and A. Schleicher, "Changes in Science Achievement: 1970–1984," in *The IEA Study of Science III: Changes in Science Education and Achievement: 1970 to 1984* (New York: Pergamon Press, 1991): 278.

19. Coulson, *Market Education*, 189–90.

20. Harold W. Stevenson and Karen Bartsch, "An Analysis of Japanese and American Textbooks in Mathematics," in *Japanese Educational Productivity* (Ann Arbor: Center for Japanese Studies of the University of Michigan, 1992): 103–33. Harold W. Stevenson and James W. Stigler, *The Learning Gap* (New York: Touchstone,

1994): 39–43. Alice Gill and Liz McPike, "What We Can Learn from Japanese Teachers' Manuals," *American Educator*, Spring 1995.

21. Eisenhower National Clearinghouse (ENC), "Japanese Education Today: An Overview of the Formal Education System," part of the ENC's set of resources for understanding and discussing TIMSS, the Third International Mathematics and Science Study. Available on-line at http://www.enc.org/TIMSS/addtools/pubs/124016/4016_11.htm. 1999.

22. Harnisch, 325, 332–33. Similar figures can be found in Dolly, 2.

23. K. Kitamura, paraphrased in Harnisch, 323.

24. T. Sawada and S. Kobayashi, paraphrased in Harnisch, 330. See also Dolly, 18.

25. Coulson, *Market Education*, Chapter 4.

26. Coulson, *Market Education*, Chapter 2.

27. The National Center on the Educational Quality of the Workforce, *The EQW National Employer Survey: First Findings* (Philadelphia: EQW, 1995).

28. Marisa Katz, "Many High School Grads Lack Job Skills," *USA Today*, May 28, 1997, D5.

29. Cited in "Reaching the Next Step," a paper jointly published by the Human Resources Development Institute of the AFL-CIO and the American Federation of Teachers. Available on the Internet at http://www.stw.ed.gov/products/600/600.htm.

30. Charles J. Sykes, *Dumbing Down Our Kids: Why American Children Feel Good About Themselves but Can't Read, Write or Add* (New York: St. Martin's Press, 1995): 22–23.

31. Gerald Strauss, "Techniques of Indoctrination: The German Reformation," in *Literacy and Social Development in the West: A Reader* (Cambridge: Cambridge University Press, 1981): 98.

32. Coulson, *Market Education*, 86–88.

33. Stanley M. Elam and Lowell C. Rose, "The 27th Annual Phi Delta Kappa/Gallup Poll of the Public's Attitudes toward the Public Schools," *Phi Delta Kappan*, Sept., 1995, 41–56.

34. In the early 1920s, all reference to the theory of evolution had been expunged from the textbooks of Florida, Louisiana, Texas, and Kentucky. Thirty-seven states introduced anti-evolution bills during the 1920s, with Arkansas, Mississippi, Tennessee, and Oklahoma passing them into law. School biology books published from the late 1920s onward ignored the theory of evolution, with later editions excising the words "evolution" and "Darwin" from their indices. More than thirty years after the Scopes case, public school science texts continued to avoid the topic of evolution. See: Coulson, *Market Education*, 123–27.

35. Coulson, *Market Education*, 81–82.
36. See Coulson, *Market Education*, Chapters 2, 3, 4, and 7.
37. Coulson, *Market Education*, 319–20.
38. Abraham Blinderman, "Medieval Correspondence Education: The Responsa of the Gaonate," *History of Education Quarterly* 9, no. 4 (1969): 471–74.
39. Nancy Kober and Diane Stark Rentner, *Do You Know the Good News about American Education?* (Washington, D.C.: Center on Education Policy and the American Youth Policy Forum, 2000).
40. Phillip Kaufman, Xianglei Chen, Susan P. Choy, Sally A. Ruddy, Amanda K. Miller, Kathryn A. Chandler, Christopher D. Chapman, Michael R. Rand, Patsy Klaus, *Indicators of School Crime and Safety 1999* (Washington, D.C.: U.S. Department of Education and U.S. Department of Justice, 1999).
41. Kaufman et al., *Indicators of School Crime*, 44.
42. Kaufman et al., *Indicators of School Crime*, 50.
43. Kaufman et al., *Indicators of School Crime*, 73.
44. Kaufman et al., *Indicators of School Crime*, 30, 72.
45. Kaufman et al., *Indicators of School Crime*, ix.
46. Coulson, *Market Education*, 268.
47. Coulson, *Market Education*, Chapter 6.
48. Coulson, *Market Education*, 276.
49. Coleman considered school systems to be highly segregated if nearly all the students of a given race or ethnicity were concentrated in a few schools, and he considered them integrated if the different races and ethnicities were evenly distributed among all the schools in a given system.
50. James Coleman, "Predicting the Consequences of Policy Changes: The Case of Public and Private Schools," in Coleman, *Equality and Achievement in Education* (Boulder, CO: Westview Press, 1990): 255–56.
51. Jay P. Greene, "Integration Where It Counts: A Study of Racial Integration in Public and Private Schools," paper presented to the American Political Science Association, Boston, September 1998.
52. Janet R. Beales and Thomas F. Bertonneau, "Do Private Schools Serve Difficult-to-Educate Students?" Mackinac Center for Public Policy, 1997.
53. Coulson, *Market Education*, 334.
54. See Bryk, Lee, and Holland, *Catholic Schools and the Common Good*. Also, Coulson, *Market Education*, Chapter 8.
55. Frank Smith, *A History of English Elementary Education 1760–1902* (London: University of London Press, 1931): 53.

56. Edward Royle, *Modern Britain, a Social History 1750–1985* (Kent: Edward Arnold, 1990): 351.
57. Alison Prentice, *The School Promoters: Education and Social Class in Mid-Nineteenth Century Upper Canada* (Toronto: McClelland and Stewart, 1988): 178.
58. Coulson, *Market Education*, Chapter 8.
59. Jay P. Greene, Joseph Giammo, and Nicole Mellow, "The Effect of Private Education on Political Participation, Social Capital, and Tolerance: An Examination of the Latino National Political Survey," working paper, University of Texas at Austin, 1998, available on-line at http://www.la.utexas.edu/research/ppc/lnps11_4. html.
60. See Coulson, *Market Education*, Chapter 8.

Competing Visions of the Child, the Family, and the School

Jennifer Roback Morse

This article suggests a new way of understanding the connections between the child, his parents, and the school. The currently dominant view of the triad of child, parents, and school focuses on the delivery of resources to children. Under this vision, the primary connection between the parents and children is the transfer of resources. The school's role is to replace material, intellectual, psychological, or moral resources that the family fails to deliver.

I propose an alternative vision. The most important role that parents play is to build a relationship with their child. The transfer of resources from parents to children is a by-product of this primary job of creating a relationship. The school's role in this scenario is to act as a partner or assistant, but not as a substitute for the parents.

This shift in vision has consequences for educational policy and for social policy more generally. Assigning primacy to the relationship over the resources implies that the public should not transfer resources to children if it undermines the parent-child relationship. At the very least, policy-makers should find some way to effect the transfer of resources that will support rather than undermine the family.

In this paper, I give reasons to believe that the primary role of the family is the building of relationships. I defend this proposition with evidence drawn from several sources. The experience of children who have no families at all demonstrates the importance of relationships relative to resources. I also draw from the evidence showing that children with disrupted parental relationships have a variety of difficulties, including problems in school. Finally, I offer examples that illustrate the impact of parental involvement on educational outcomes.

Debating on the turf labeled "transferring resources from big people to little people" stacks the deck in favor of an intrusive public policy regarding children. Changing the terms of the debate to "building up the relationships inside the family" reveals that there are costs to indiscriminately assigning quasi-parental authority to public agencies, including schools. Focusing on the relational aspect of the family also points the direction toward policy options that are scarcely even on today's policy agenda.

CURRENT POLICIES THAT TRANSFER RESOURCES WHILE UNDERMINING THE FAMILY

It may seem a bit hysterical to conceive of the present policy paradigm as attempting to supply resources the family fails to deliver. Here are just a few of the many policies and recent proposals with exactly that thrust. Not only do these policies replace parental resources with public resources, there is good reason to expect that these policies will weaken the relationship between parents and children, rather than build it up.

Universal Preschool

In October 1999, the Department of Education released a study of 111 very poor children. The study concluded that an intensive early intervention preschool program improved their chances of going to college. The academics who conducted this study and the Department of Education, which funded it, used this research as an argument for universal day care beginning in infancy. Some advocates of universal day care go so far as to claim that it will be a cost-effective crime-control program.[1]

Universal day care means care for the children of well-educated professionals, and for the children of dedicated working-class parents who sacrifice to keep an adult in the home all day. The study had absolutely nothing to say about the impact of preschool on these populations, since the test group was a group whose parents were extremely poor and uneducated.

Universal School Breakfast Program

In May 2000, the federal government approved a pilot study designed to test the question whether children's school performance is improved by providing all children of all income levels a free breakfast at school. The proponent of the study, Rep. Lynn Woolsey, predicted the outcome of the study: providing a free breakfast for all students will prove to be a wise educational investment and a better way to care for children. "We know that a good breakfast is as necessary to a good education as are books, pencils or computers. . . . (Public schools) don't ask wealthy children to pay for books or supplies," and she maintained they should take the same approach to school breakfast. One proponent said, "We think that just because there is food in the refrigerator (at home) that a child is going to eat breakfast," as an argument that even well-off parents cannot be counted on to feed their children breakfast.[2]

So, in an era of unprecedented prosperity, the state proposes to take over one of the most primal functions of the family, to feed its own young.

Berkeley Sues Home School Parents

In June 2000, bureaucrats at California's Berkeley Unified School District brought proceedings against four families there who homeschool their children. When the families were summoned to a truancy hearing at which they declined to provide attendance records or curriculum information, they were referred to the Alameda County District Attorney for contributing to the delinquency of minors. The families contended, however, that refusing to present documents is their right under the California Education Code.

It is hard to imagine a deeper commitment to the welfare of one's child than the commitment to educate them at home. Yet, the educational authorities are spending time and resources attacking these dedicated families. Observers say that money is behind the most recent attack. Schools are reimbursed by the state according to their average daily attendance. The more pupils—including homeschoolers who might be lassoed in—the more money the school gets, the more teachers to be hired, the more union members recruited, and the more union dues collected.[3]

Besides these recent headlines, policymakers over the last generation have called upon the schools to provide an increasing array of noneducational services. Some schools teach things as mundane as toothbrushing and personal hygiene. Many schools have on-site day care centers, offering care before and after school. It isn't unusual for schools to sponsor various kinds of health-screening services, such as vision screening. Some elected officials advocate publicly funded health clinics on school grounds, where students can receive medical care without parental consent or knowledge.

Besides these instances of schools providing basic care for children, many schools have expanded their curriculum to include topics once universally regarded as the domain of the family. Sex education teaches children "the facts of life," while "death education" teaches them the facts of death. Schools have implemented "values clarification" programs as substitutes for parental instruction in morals. Many parents believe that these programs work at cross purposes with their own objectives of teaching good moral behavior. Parents have sometimes found it difficult to remove their own children from these courses, much less to get the school to change the curriculum altogether.[4]

Thus, the schools have become suppliers of resources to children, often in opposition to the interests or wishes of the family. It is hardly alarmist to observe that, whatever their intentions, many policymakers have placed the school in the position of substituting for family resources. The question of whether policies such as these support or undermine the family is hardly ever raised, much less considered decisive.

Many critics of these trends focus on what might be called "the academic crowding-out effect." Time spent teaching values clarification or toothbrushing is time that cannot be spent teaching math or phonics. I take a different approach. I focus on the "family crowding-out effect." The time that children spend in school is time taken away from the family. The responsibilities taken over by the schools are responsibilities that no longer fall upon the family.

The primary duty of parents is to build relationships with their children. Building relationships requires time, above all. The responsibilities of parents toward their children are a vital part of the web of connections between them. Eating together, doing chores together, sometimes just doing nothing together; these are all part of being in a relationship with another person. In the process of being together, children learn to trust their parents as a source of sustenance as well as information, guidance, and protection. These connections and the trust that flows from them prepare children to be in other, more distant, relationships that also require trust and trustworthy behavior.[5]

Giving explicit moral instruction is only a small part of how parents impart information about how to behave decently. Children obtain this kind of moral knowledge by the example of how their parents live. Seeing their parents and participating with them in all kinds of activities is a part of that process. As the state takes over the time parents spend with children and the responsibilities that parents owe to children, it diminishes the opportunities for building connections inside the family. If parents fail to build bonds with their children, the benefits cannot so easily be replaced by schools.

To see why the parent-child relationship is so important, and how unlikely it is to be replaced, we turn to a discussion of children without any relationships at all: children who were raised in eastern European orphanages.

CHILDREN WITH NO RELATIONSHIPS

Understanding the problems of the abandoned infant shows how many and subtle are the ways in which a loving family influences a child's development. Mothers and babies do more together than we can easily replace through even the most expansive or best-funded public policies.

Orphanage workers and developmental pediatricians report the "failure to thrive" syndrome observed in minimal-care orphanages. Children who are deprived of human contact during infancy sometimes fail to gain weight and to develop, even though all the bodily, material needs of the child are met.[6] The children who survive infancy in the orphanage frequently have sensory-integration problems. The children cannot successfully integrate incoming sensory information, so they are overwhelmed by sounds, sights, and tactile sensations.[7] Children with auditory-processing disorder frequently score adequately on standard picture vocabulary tests of the kind given to preschoolers, but they have difficulty responding to multiple commands, answering questions or performing tasks that require sequencing information.[8]

The tactile system of the body helps to determine where on the body the person is being touched and what is touching them. This can be a protective system that triggers the fight or flight response when dangerous sensations are registered.[9] The vestibular sense of the body gives a child information about where his head is in relation to solid ground. This sense tells a child about movement and gravity. The proprioceptive sense relates to the child's sense of body position. This is the system that lets us know the relative position of our body parts, without the use of our vision.[10]

Because these basic bodily senses are the foundation for an array of motor and coordination skills, these children have a surprising array of developmental and educational problems.

These kids are hampered in their ability to do motor planning for activities as simple as crawling, pedaling a bicycle, or using stairs. They might have trouble with simple tasks that require coordinating both sides of the body, such as catching a large ball, using a rolling pin, or tying shoes. Such a child may have difficulty with pencil and paper tasks required in elementary school. Even holding the pencil may be a problem, much less coordinating the hands with the eyes. The child may find it difficult to sit at a desk for very long because he is continually aware of the tactile input he gets just from sitting.[11]

The most surprising deficit correlated with sensory-integration problems is a difficulty with speech and language development. The connection had been noted by American researcher A. Jean Ayers,[12] who discovered that spinning or rocking a child can sometimes enhance his ability to develop speech and language. The connection was strengthened by the observations of eastern European orphans who exhibited both extreme sensory integration and language difficulties.

For children raised in normal families, the sensory systems develop in the ordinary course of life. Adults pick up the child, hold him, rock him, tickle him, and play with him. In these earliest months, the child learns primarily through bodily or motor processes, rather than intellectual or cognitive processes. When daddies and big brothers toss the baby in the air, or give her an airplane ride, or spin her around, they are, whether they realize it or not, stimulating the vestibular and the proprioceptive bodily-movement systems. In a pathetic attempt to take care of themselves, many post-institutionalized children stimulate themselves by spinning and rocking, at an age when most children have outgrown the need to be rocked.

THE SIGNIFICANCE OF THE NEGLECTED INFANT

Reflecting on the myriad difficulties of the abandoned infant suggests transferring resources is certainly not the best way to understand what goes on between mothers and babies. The losses these children sustain are so numerous, so profound, and so resistant to correction that they require thousands of dollars, and hundreds of hours of highly trained specialists from numerous disciplines just to bring the child back to a very low threshold of normal functioning. Needless to say, the resources needed to repair this damage far exceed any reasonable value we might place on the mother's time, even the fulltime commitment of a highly educated and highly paid mother.

Reflecting on the neglected infant also helps us appreciate the surprising importance of the simple activities that parents do with their babies. Most parents rock their babies and look into their eyes, without realizing that this activity wards off attachment disorder. Very few parents are conscious of the fact that they are stimulating their baby's vestibular and proprioceptive systems when they bounce the baby on their knees, or pick them up above the head and wiggle them. Most parents don't realize that they are teaching their child basic trust and reciprocity every time they play peek-a-boo. People have been playing patty-cake with babies for generations without realizing that this simple game stimulates the development of motor planning and coordination.

We can apply one of the great insights of the theory of free societies to this intricate set of interactions between parents and children. Frederick Hayek argued that free economies would outperform centrally planned economies. The free, decentralized economy uses the local information and tacit knowledge of particular times and circumstances. He argued further that a centrally planned economy could never gather this information, no matter how aggressive the data-gathering collection procedures, no matter how sophisticated the computers.[13]

In a specialized economy, people become highly focused on the particular thing they produce. They have a tremendous amount of knowledge about their own little corner of the world, both literally and figuratively. They know their specialty and their locality. Much of this knowledge is tacit, not explicit. People routinely use knowledge they can barely articulate. They might be able to describe what they do and why in broad outlines. But a large percentage of their activities defy the kind of description that is detailed enough to be useful to a far-away planning commissar.

In a free society, people use this information because it is in their interest to do the best job they can do, even if they can't fully explain how and why they do it. A lot of information is generated and carried by the prices in a free economy. Very few people stop to reflect upon exactly what goes into the making of prices, even of products they use every day. Hayek argued that the attempt to replace the decentralized price system with a centrally planned, command economy would squander all this information.

There is a very strong analogy with the work of parenthood. Most parents cannot articulate the physiological and psychological significance of the activities they do with their children. Indeed, if you ask the mother of an infant what she did all day, she is unlikely to be able to even describe her activities, except in the most general way. She might tell you how many times she changed his diaper. But she will probably forget to mention that she looked in the baby's eyes, wiggled his toes, and laughed while she imitated his baby babbling sounds. She might tell you she folded laundry and did dishes. But she probably won't remember that she rewarded every little noise her baby made, by smiling at the baby, or imitating the baby's sound, or having an imaginary conversation with him. Far more work is going on in a normal mother-infant pair than we would ever have imagined, in the absence of the horrendous counterexample provided by our little eastern European orphans.

Parents naturally know more about their particular child than even the most dedicated professional. Parents care about the welfare of their child and will go out of their way to pursue it. We cannot reasonably expect professional educators, psychologists, doctors, or any other specialists to care in the same way. The knowledge that specialists can provide has to be used by someone who specializes in the specific case of this particular child. Parents are in a position to know whether their child is responding well to a particular specialized course of study or medical treatment. The child needs the parent to run the gauntlet of the experts to sift the appropriate from the inapplicable.

This is the work we are risking when we attempt to replace the family with institutions. The further down that path we go, the more we risk. I do not mean to say that there is a one-to-one connection between each and every one of these syndromes and an increase in nonmaternal care. I do not mean to suggest that children in American day cares are at an increased risk for each and every one of these problems, still less that children in public schools are at higher risks for such syndromes. I do mean to say that when Horace Mann and John Dewey set us off down this road of sequestering children in age-segregated institutions, we had no idea what was at the end of that road.

Reflecting on the neglected infant illustrates the primacy of relationship-building in the child's life, as well as the improbability of replacing all the work of the family by a mere transfer of resources. We turn now to another sort of evidence about the importance of relationships for the child's development: the evidence from American families with disrupted relationships. This material is immediately relevant to education policy because we can see a close connection between broken relationships and school performance.

CHILDREN WITH BROKEN RELATIONSHIPS

By now, social scientists have accumulated an impressive body of evidence showing the educational and emotional difficulties that children in single-parent families, and even stepfamilies, face.[14] One review of studies found that children from mother-only families obtain fewer years of education and are more likely to drop out of high school. Offspring from mother-only families are more likely to commit delinquent acts and to engage in drug and alcohol use than offspring from two-parent families.[15] The lower incomes of single-parent families account for only a portion of the differences between mother-only families and two-parent families. The effects of single motherhood are consistent across a large number of racial and ethnic groups.[16]

Children of single parents are more likely to have academic problems. Children from disrupted marriages were over 70 percent more likely than those living with both biological parents to have been expelled or suspended: those living with never-married mothers were more than twice as likely to have had this experience. Children with both biological parents were less likely to have repeated a grade of school.[17]

Mother-only families may create spillover effects on other children in the schools.[18] One recent study, using a nationally representative sample of over 20,000 eighth-graders from 970 schools, took account of parental income and education, and the mean level of socioeconomic status of the families attending the school. Being in a single-parent family not only lowered a child's math score, but also had an impact on other students. Students who attended schools with a high concentration of students from single-parent households had math and reading achievement scores that were 11 percent and 10 percent, respectively, lower than students who attended schools with a higher concentration of two-parent households.

Children living in single-parent households are also more likely to have emotional and behavioral problems. The children outside of two-parent families had 50–80 percent higher scores for indicators of antisocial behavior, peer conflict, social withdrawal, and age-inappropriate dependency. Such children also had 25–50 percent higher scores for indicators of anxiety, depression, headstrong behavior, and hyperactivity.[19] These conditions, if serious enough, can land a child in special education classes.

One might think that replacing the absent father with a new man would alleviate some of the children's difficulties. A stepfather typically does bring additional income to the family and potentially could increase the amount of adult time and attention the children receive. But, consistent with the hypothesis that relationships are more important than increased resources, introducing a "new father" into the picture does not necessarily solve the child's problems, and may add some new ones.

The psychological adjustment and educational achievement of children in stepfamilies is similar to that of children in one-parent families.[20] For instance, children with stepfathers have approximately the same high risk of repeating a year of school as do the children of never-married mothers, around 75 percent. The increase in risk was 40 percent for children of divorced mothers.[21] A recent study found that when a stepfather enters the home, children exhibit more behavior problems compared to their peers who live with both biological parents, and the impact is slightly stronger for boys than for girls.[22]

Another recent study tried to capture the effects of father involvement on "home problems" and "school problems." The study found that more involvement by any type of father, including a stepfather, reduces both problems at home and in the school.[23] However, the study also showed that stepfathers are less involved with the children. The presence of a stepfather is correlated with less involvement from the mother. Since mother's involvement correlates with fewer child problems, the presence of a stepfather in effect delivers a double whammy to the kids. Stepfathers spend less time with children than biological fathers, and a stepfather reduces the time mothers spend with their children.[24]

These problems can translate into lowered academic achievement. One study specifically examined the relationship of family structure, time spent with kids, and academic achievement.[25] Children in two-parent families got the highest grades of any family structure. The time fathers, stepfathers, and biological fathers alike spent with children had a positive impact on their grades. However, because stepfathers spend so much less time with kids than do dads in two-parent families, family structure still has a significant impact on grades.

This evidence is consistent with the major premise of this article: children need relationships more than they need resources, and satisfying the child's relationship needs translates into better academic performance. Children raised in fatherless homes have lower academic achievement, even controlling for the lower incomes of two-parent families. Children in stepfamilies have difficulties, despite the availability of greater adult resources within the family. The relationships, on average, simply are not strong enough to supply the needs that children have.

Virtually all researchers accept the correlation between higher academic achievement and living with both biological parents, because this correlation is present in the raw data of so many studies. The debate among the scholars centers on how much of the difference in academic performance can be accounted for by differences in resources typically found in single-parent households.

I propose that we shift the terms of this debate. It is certainly an admirable impulse to try to increase the resources available to poorer children, but most studies show that some differences in performance remain even after accounting for differences in economic resources. This suggests that the children are harmed by the loss of relationship itself, not simply the loss of resources.

We can begin to do two kinds of things differently. First, we can drop the posture of neutrality among family types, which flies in the face of so much evidence. We need to be willing to see the connection between the decisions of parents to marry or not, or to divorce or not, and the academic performance of the children. It is almost as if policymakers wish they could find any way possible to help the children, short of stating the obvious fact that they would be better off if their parents were married. The premise seems to be: what is the minimal set of human relationships that a child can have and still turn out tolerably well?

This minimalist mentality shows up in the conclusions people draw from studies of the impact of the father's time. Of course, children would benefit from more time and attention from their fathers. It is perfectly appropriate to encourage fathers, including stepfathers, to spend more time with children. But we are not justified in drawing the conclusion that there is no reason to be concerned about family structure as long as stepfathers spend enough time with their stepchildren.

A similar analysis applies to the debates over support for low-income single mothers, and proposals to crack down on "deadbeat dads." The idea of making sure that single mothers have adequate resources with which to raise their children is certainly reasonable. But it does not follow that the children would be fine in a one-parent household if only the income of that household were high enough.

Many people seem to believe that it is unreasonable to encourage people to get married and stay married. But asking stepfathers to behave like biological fathers may be every bit as difficult a burden. Stepfathers behave systematically differently from biological fathers. It is unrealistic to expect a man to work as hard on a relationship with another man's child as he would with his own child. Nor is it realistic to expect that a father who has been expelled from his home in a nasty divorce will ante up the same amount of money that he would naturally contribute if he were part of a functioning family. It is more straightforward, as well as more sensible, to expect men and women to work together to maintain their marriage relationships in the first place.

This leads to the second way the terms of the debate need to change. We need to stop allowing the minimalist position to go unchallenged. Conservatives used to be accused of minimalism regarding money. Conservative demands for fiscal accountability were frequently countered with the accusation: "You want to spend the least money necessary for getting tolerable educational results."

I don't think anyone seriously believes that this is the issue dividing conservatives and liberals on education anymore. But many people, from both the right and the left, seem to be willing to adopt a minimalist position with regard to relationships and their impact on children. We seem to be asking, what do I have to do in order to maintain my position that divorce or single-parenthood is not harmful to children? How much money does society have to spend from outside the family to make up for the loss of relationship, so that I won't have to give up my belief that parents are entitled to any lifestyle choices they want? We should confront these relationship issues with more generosity toward the children, rather than asking how little we must do.

Kids with no relationships at all have a terrible time. Kids with disrupted relationships have problems. I propose that we investigate ways to involve the parents more, to use the knowledge and motivation that parents naturally have. Rather than focus on correcting the defects of the worst parents, we should focus on fostering the efforts of the vast majority of ordinary parents, who are perfectly adequate.

CHILDREN WITH PRETTY-GOOD RELATIONSHIPS WITH GOOD-ENOUGH PARENTS

No one would argue with the proposition that parents ought to be more involved with their children's education. But one might ask whether it is really practical to ask parents to become more active in the educational lives of their children. Recent studies offer grounds for believing both that additional parental involvement is beneficial to children's academic achievement and that even parents of modest means can become more involved.

For instance, a recent study of 10,000 high school students in Wisconsin and California examined the impact of parental involvement in a child's schooling on the child's grades.[26] Parental involvement was a composite measure of five items: whether parents attend school programs for parents, watch the students in sports or activities, help choose courses, help with homework when asked, and monitor school progress. An increased level of involvement by either mothers or fathers improved student grade-point averages. This held true across lines of income, race, and parental education levels. In fact, the author concludes, "higher levels of school involvement had the same benefit on grades, irrespective of parents' education or the type of family structure."[27]

This author cites earlier studies that "demonstrated the feasibility of teaching high-risk parents or parents with limited English proficiency to become involved in the schooling of elementary or high school students and documented how this involvement, in turn, benefited their children's performance (Simich-Dudgeon 1993: Smith 1968). These studies suggest that parental school involvement is a malleable parenting practice."[28]

Another study examined the impact of parental involvement on eighth-grade math and reading scores. The study found that having a parent who "discusses school matters" has as great an impact on improving both math and reading scores, as does having a parent with a higher level of education.[29] Taken together, these works give reason to believe that parental involvement by parents of low education or income is just as valuable to their children as involvement by parents with more education or income. And, parents can be persuaded to become more involved.

James Coleman's concept of "social capital" also explains differences in school performance.[30] Social capital in the home concerns the relationships between the child and his or her own parents. One way of understanding the problems of single-parent families is that these families have lower levels of social capital.[31] Social capital within the wider community of the school concerns the wider web of social networks and relationships. Coleman used this notion of social capital to account for the superior academic performance of students in Catholic high schools over public schools. Coleman argued that Catholic schools provided a richer, more dense network of social connections than public schools.[32]

The previously cited study of eighth-grade reading and math scores tested Coleman's thesis by using information about individual students and their families, as well as information about the school. Parents were asked about their involvement in their child's school, as well as their interaction with other parents in the school. The question asked of the parents was: how many parents of your child's friends do you know? This measure was called "parental social relations" or "parental acquaintances."[33]

This study reported impressive effects on academic performance from the social environment of the school, as measured by mean number of parental acquaintances. More parental interaction with other parents increases the average math and reading scores of the school. These effects persist even after controlling for the average socioeconomic status of the families attending the school. In other words, the benefits from creating rich social networks among parents can accrue to schools in poor neighborhoods, as well as in more affluent ones.

Parents can also help their children by having high expectations for their performance. Some of the studies of this issue are suspect, however, because they conflate the effects of parental prediction and parental ambition. The question, "What do you think your child's grade in math will be?" may simply be tracking the parents' knowledge of their child's likely performance, rather than the parents' goals for the child.

Nevertheless, some measures of parental expectations covary with specific actions that parents choose to take. According to one author, "data from the Beginning School Study show that parents who expect their child to do well in school are more likely than others to provide books and academic games, read to the child, and take the child to the library. These kinds of activities, at least for young children, are almost as easy for parents of limited means to do as they are for parents who are more affluent."[34] Encouraging parents to engage in these kinds of activities with their children seems like a reasonable effort, whatever interpretive difficulties the variable "parental expectations" may present.

Finally, some of the preschool demonstration projects used to argue for universal day care actually have elements that support the idea of working with parents, rather than using the preschool as a substitute for care inside the family. The more sophisticated and lavishly funded of the early-intervention preschool programs intervene with parents as well as with children. Some have parent-education components, including home visits. Others have requirements that the parents contribute to the preschool program by doing activities such as being classroom aides, accompanying field trips or organizing resources in the classroom. In a variety of programs from Chicago, North Carolina, Birmingham, New Orleans, and Houston, the involvement of the parents exerted a beneficial influence on the outcome, independently of the activities of the preschool itself.[35] Given the mixed results of preschool and early intervention programs overall, we may well wonder whether the crucial variable of helping the family might be the most direct way to do lasting good for children.

POLICY IMPLICATIONS

Family relationships are important to the well-being of children, including their educational achievement. Changing the policy perspective from transferring resources to building the family adds a new twist to many current debates and brings some new policies into focus.

THE SCHOOL-CHOICE DEBATE

Emphasizing family involvement and family relationships adds a dimension to the school-choice debate. School-choice programs are likely to induce parents to become more involved with their children's education. A parent with a voucher is much less likely to simply go on autopilot and enroll her child in the nearest public school. For many parents, having a voucher in hand will be the first time they have had to think through the question of which school is best for their children. The current situation of little or no choice encourages parental passivity, which cannot be good for the relationship between the parents and childen.

In fact, encouraging parents to be more active on behalf of their children could be one of the features that shapes the details of a school-choice plan. Some choice plans require parents to specifically opt out of the public school system. Charter schools are an example of this. In principle, any parent can petition to start a charter school. In practice, however, it is so much easier to remain with the status quo that many parents continue to be complacent. All parents have a choice, but it is possible and quite a bit easier for parents to continue with the local public school. Most voucher plans, by contrast, allow the public schools as a choice but require every parent to make a specific decision to remain in, or opt out of, the neighborhood public school. The activation of the parents should be considered an advantage of such a program. Tax credit programs are somewhere in between charter schools and vouchers in terms of mobilizing parents. If a parent chooses a school that charges tuition, then the parent receives a tax credit. But the path of least resistance may very well be to stick with the familiar, tuition-free local public school.

No parental choice program can guarantee, of course, that parents will think the school decision through well or without error. But over time, parents themselves will begin to receive the feedback they need to make better decisions. The parents, who are the nearest to the children, will see whether the school is meeting their educational and other needs. The parent will have a greater incentive to monitor these situations more closely than they now do. Most people find it painful to gather a lot of information about a situation they have no power to control or change.

But more is at stake than being informed about education itself. Parents who are in command of this key decision in their child's life are learning to be more engaged with their children generally. Look at it this way: the current system requires parents to deposit their children with strangers for at least six hours a day, five days a week. Parents have very little, if any, influence over the content of the instruction, the identity of the instructor, the behavior of the peer group, or the rules of the classroom. Parents are more or less required to acquiesce in whatever goes on in school. Is it any wonder that parents become passive?

CROWDING OUT THE FAMILY

Policymakers should ask themselves how their proposals will impact the relationships inside the family. The work that goes on inside the family is frequently subtle and intangible, often difficult to measure, or even to fully articulate. The tacit knowledge that families have of their own children will be difficult to replicate. This point is reminiscent of Hayek's critique of centrally planned economies and should have the same humbling influence. With this thought in mind, we should set more modest goals for public policy.

For example, day care enthusiasts hope that paid care-givers can substitute for the work that parents do with in-fants and preschoolers. Some studies show that some children, usually girls, benefit from the preschool experience. These studies track a couple of measurable indicators of things such as language development or cognitive skills.[36]

But, when other researchers attempt to study more subtle things such as children's behavior, or the quality of the at-tachment between children and their parents, the case for day care is not nearly so rosy.[37] There are complex interreactions between the quality of care and the sensitivity of the mother to her child. It appears that children of less sensitive or less responsive mothers are at higher risk for being insecurely at-tached to their mothers. This risk is greater if these children are in low quality, rather than high quality, day care. That is, high quality care out of the home seems to buffer some of the effects of maternal insensitivity. But, perhaps surprisingly, these same children are more likely to be insecurely attached, the more hours they spend in out-of-home day care. Re-searchers hypothesize that these children need more time with their mothers "to develop the internalized sense that their mothers are responsive and available to them."[38]

Studies tracking children as they mature through the preschool years give reason to believe that day care children become more aggressive. Children in nonmaternal care during their first year of life do not necessarily behave differently during that year. But the children cared for outside the home in their first year are more likely to be aggressive during the second and possibly later years as well.[39] The researchers do not have a complete explanation for what they have observed. But the fact that they cannot completely explain it illustrates how complex the developmental process really is, and cautions us about visionary schemes for completely replacing maternal care.

Finally, studies of day care consistently show that higher quality day care produces outcomes superior to those of lower quality day care. The impact of low-quality day care is particularly pronounced when the mother is less sensitive or responsive to her child. It seems reasonable to suppose that lower income families purchase lower quality child care, on average, simply because of their budget constraints. Yet no study that I have seen shows a consistent relationship between maternal insensitivity and income. The children of the poor might very well benefit more from increased time with their mothers than from more time in low quality day care. If so, the policy focus should shift away from increasing the quality of day care to increasing the ability of lower income families to keep one adult at home to care for the children. Increased tax credits specifically targeted to lower income families could be one way of accomplishing this.

The proposal for universal school breakfasts offers another example of a policy that will have subtle effects on the family. Advocates are counting on stressed-out, over-worked, two-earner couples to offer political support for extending a program that now serves only the financially indigent. The public argument focuses on the benefits of guaranteeing that every child begins the school day with a nutritious breakfast. But it is not difficult to see the subtext: providing breakfast at school will be convenient for all parents, especially working parents.

Even the most highly paid families could be persuaded by the convenience, which is the real selling point of the program.

But we are losing something important, though intangible, when we put comfort first. Eating meals together is one of the focal points of family life. People talk to each other. People share. The family members get some time together. Children see their parents as people who provide nourishment to them. Children learn table manners. Even at breakfast, when people may be eating in shifts, family members have the opportunity for some time together. It is unrealistic to believe that the only thing that goes on during a meal is the ingestion of calories.

Critics may respond that this is an idealized picture. People are too busy to eat together. Children are too disrespectful and jaded to sit still through a family meal. Besides, breakfast isn't the place for that kind of family unity. Dinner is the time when most families do that kind of bonding. Many families have even given up on eating dinner together. Breakfast can easily fall between the cracks.

Kids missing breakfast once in a while is no big deal. But if it happens habitually, most families see that something is wrong. Every family approaches this kind of problem differently, because every family has a little bit different story and different priorities. Some people work out new car pools or transportation arrangements. For some families, the main problem is how to get some of the family members closer to home. Some families are able to reduce the working hours of one adult, so that at least one person has the time to keep the home front running more smoothly. Other families decide that keeping one of the adults at home is the highest priority.

A universal school-breakfast program enables people to avoid this entire line of reflection and problem-solving. The federal government, using the local public schools, would be subsidizing people at their most chaotic. Besides, not every family has two earners and two kids dashing madly out the door without breakfast. A great many families have put some time and effort into making sure its members eat in some semblance of peace and order. Those families would probably end up using the school-breakfast program, if it were low cost enough and handy enough, just as most families now use the subsidized school-lunch program. The convenience of the program, which is a selling point for the stressed-out family, will disrupt and displace the efforts of the conscientious family.

POLICIES THAT ENCOURAGE FAMILY INVOLVEMENT WITH SCHOOLS

This brings up another whole realm of possible policies that are not even being discussed: policies that build family involvement with children, specifically in their lives at school. I recall from my childhood that my little parochial school served a hot lunch. The kitchen staff consisted of two employees and a rotating team of four parent volunteers. Once a month, my mom and three of her friends from our neighborhood helped serve lunch at school. I cannot claim that her monthly presence improved my academic achievement. But it surely increased the likelihood that she knew what was going on with me at school. And from the children's point of view, what a delight it was for all of us, to see our mothers behind the cafeteria line!

This was not a parish filled with wealthy or sophisticated people. These were working-class families, who struggled to make ends meet. Somehow, those working-class mothers managed to get us off to school with breakfast in our stomachs. Somehow, our school principal and parish priest induced them to contribute to the good of the community by showing up once a month to help in the cafeteria.

Many non-public schools have parental participation as a requirement of a child's attendance. Whether it is a cooperative preschool run in a church basement, or an elite prep school, many schools rely on various kinds of inputs from parents. Sometimes, parents do mundane things like helping repair and maintain school property. Other parents are involved directly in the classroom, as teachers' aides, as tutors for particular children, or instructors in specialized subjects. Virtually all private schools engage the assistance of parents in fund-raising activities. Some fund-raising activities are strictly financial affairs, such as capital campaign drives, whereas others are real community-building enterprises. Most schools are well aware that their bake sales and festivals and spaghetti dinners build up an esprit de corps that has spillover benefits to the school.

Public schools currently use parent volunteers only on a sporadic basis. Sometimes the call for volunteers is perfunctory. Whether the parents who volunteer are fully utilized depends on the temperament of the particular teacher. Teachers are not really trained to engage the parents or use them effectively.

Local public schools could begin to experiment with parental participation requirements. Many schools now require parents to sign their children's homework folder in order for the child to get full credit for doing the homework. This is, obviously, a very minimal requirement for parental supervision and involvement. But it is something, and it should be expanded upon. Many public schools ask parents to help with fund-raising, but with little else. Certainly, few public schools have a role for parents in the ordinary work of the school or in the choice of curriculum. Schools could require parents to contribute a certain number of volunteer hours and make a variety of times available to accommodate different schedules. Schools could require parents to come in to the school to pick up their child's report card.

Some schools might find a role for parents as mentors to other parents. Teachers are often aware that a child has some problem at home, or that the child would benefit from some particular help from his parents. It isn't unusual for the teacher to find it awkward to approach the parent to tell him the child needs help. Sometimes a parent would respond differently to encouragement from another parent than from the teacher or other authority figure. This may be the kind of "social capital" that some of the previously cited studies captured. The network of parental friends and acquaintances within the school makes it more natural for parents to receive moderately "bad news" about their children, before it turns into disastrous news.

Any policies that keep the parents coming and going to the school on a regular basis are beneficial in this regard. Something as simple as having a place for parents to chat while they wait to pick up their kids after school could build up friendships among parents.

FAMILY POLICY IS EDUCATIONAL POLICY

The final policy implication of placing relationships before resources is that we must evaluate policies, that affect the family differently than we now do. Policies that affect the family are educational policies whether we like it or not, whether we admit it or not. A variety of policies have been advocated to help reduce the incidence of divorce and to restore public understanding of the importance of married-couple families. Some of these policies are modest, such as creating a public health campaign to inform people about the long-term benefits of marriage and the risks associated with divorce. Others are more ambitious, such as ending no-fault divorce for couples with children under 18, or providing a one-time tax credit to always-married couples when their youngest children reach eighteen.[40] In any case, the positive impact of married-couple families on the educational outcomes of their children needs to be considered as one of the benefits of any and all proposals that affect the family.

CONCLUSION

This, then, is the conflict of visions. Is the primary function of the family transferring resources from big people to little people? Or is the primary function of the family building relationships between mother, father, and children? The answers to these questions set the stage for a whole range of policy choices.

Free societies work well because they harness more of the efforts of more ordinary people than any social system that has yet been devised. Free economic systems work well because they harness the information that ordinary people have about their particular, localized circumstances, as Hayek argued so long ago. At the same time, free economic systems harness the motivations of more ordinary people than can a centrally planned system. More people will work harder, and more effectively, when they are pursuing their own good, and the good of their families, than they will if authorities are trying to force them all to contribute to some grand master plan.

Involving parents more heavily in their children's education should be the first priority for educational policy. The parents have both the knowledge and the motivation to do what is best for their own children. Being in a relationship with the parents is more important to the child's development than the transfers of resources that educational policy is in a position to make. Moreover, we need to be mindful that government or schools can undermine the family, by replacing its functions, by inducing parental passivity, or by actively attacking the family's values.

America needs to re-moralize the family in order to revitalize the school. First, we should drop the posture of agnostic neutrality about family types. We should stop implicitly encouraging family-types and behaviors that are destructive to children and ultimately costly to the educational system. We have had a generation or more of social experimentation and the results are in. Second, we should renew our appreciation of the relational quality of the family. We will come to have more modest expectations from public policy overall. But, we will become more impressed by the contributions that ordinary people of modest means can make to the well-being of their own children.

NOTES

1. "Superior Day Care Linked to Higher Adult Achievement," *San Jose Mercury News*, Oct. 22, 1999; "Study: Intensive, Early Education Has Long-lasting Results," Associated Press, Oct. 21, 1999; Jennifer Roback Morse, "Government Nannies," *Forbes*, March 6, 2000; "The War on Mom," Ben Boychuck and Matthew Robinson, *Washington Times*, June 2, 2000; "Child Care for Cutting Off Crime?" Benjamin P. Tyree, *Washington Times*, June 1, 2000.

2. "SR Part of Breakfast Study," *Santa Rosa Press Democrat*, May 17, 2000: B-1, 2.

3. "Brave New Schools: Home Education Banned in Berkeley?" *World Net Daily*, June 3, 2000; http://www.worldnetdaily.com/bluesky_fosterj_news/20000603_xnfoj_home_educa.shtml Cathy Cuthbert (California Homeschool Network), "Berkeley's Crusade: Educrats Target Home Schoolers with Truancy Suits," *Investor's Business Daily*, June 20, 2000. (Summarized in National Center for Policy Analysis, *News Digest*, June 21, 2000.)

4. Thomas Sowell, *Inside American Education: The Decline, The Deception, The Dogmas* (New York: The Free Press, 1993): 36–38.

5. Jennifer Roback Morse, *Love and Economics: Why the Laissez-Faire Family Doesn't Work* (Dallas: Spence Publishing, 2001), shows that free societies depend on the strength of these early trust relationships. The smooth functioning of a market economy and a self-governing political order require a large percentage of the population to trust and be trustworthy.

6. This syndrome is known as the Kaspar Hauser syndrome, or psychosocial dwarfism. See Harold I. Kaplan, M.D. and Benjamin J. Sadock, M.D., eds., *Comprehensive Textbook of Psychiatry*/VI, vol. 2, sixth edition (Baltimore: Williams and Wilkins), Chapter 40 and sections 43.3, 47.3.

7. A. Jean Ayres, *Sensory Integration and the Child* (Los Angeles, CA: Western Psychological Services, 1979) and *Sensory Integration and Learning Disorders* (Los Angeles, CA: Western Psychological Services, 1973). One expert likens a disorganized flow of sensations to life in a rush-hour traffic jam. A child who cannot organize incoming sensory information is frequently overwhelmed, especially by noise and touch.

8. "Central Auditory Processing Disorder," *The Post, The Newsletter of the Parent Network for the Post-Institutionalized Child*, Spring 1995: 5–6.

9. Gale Haradon, "Sensory Integration Therapy and Children from Deprivational Environments," in Thais Tepper, Lois Hannon and Dorothy Sandstrom, eds, *International Adoption: Challenges and Opportunities* (Meadow Lands, PA: Parent Network for the Post-Institutionalized Child, 1999): 89–92.

10. See Ayres general. See also Carol Stock Kronowitz, "Catching Preschoolers Before They Fall: A Developmental Screening," *Child Care Information Exchange*, March 1992, 25–29.

11. Gale Haradon, "Sensory Integration Therapy and Children from Deprivational Environments," in Tepper, Hannon, and Sandstrom, eds., *International Adoption* (Meadow Lands, PA: Parent Network for the Post-Institutionalized Child, 1999): 89–92.

12. See Ayres, both works cited.

13. Frederick A. Hayek, "The Use of Knowledge in Society," *American Economic Review* 35, no. 4 (1945): 519–30; *Law, Legislation and Liberty*, vol. 1, *Rules and Order* (Chicago: University of Chicago Press, 1973).

14. For the reader interested in an overview of the data and the issues, two good general sources are David Blankenhorn, *Fatherless America: Confronting Our Most Urgent Social Problem* (New York: HarperCollins, 1995), and Patrick F. Fagan and Robert Rector, "The Effects of Divorce on America," *The Heritage Foundation Backgrounder*, no. 1373, Washington, D.C., June 5, 2000.

15. Sara McLanahan and Karen Booth, "Mother-Only Families: Problems, Prospects and Politics," *Journal of Marriage and the Family* 51, no. 3 (August 1989): 557–80, reviews the relevant literature. Irwin Garfinkel and Sara S. McLanahan, *Single Mothers and Their Children* (Washington, D.C.: Urban Institute Press, 1986) pages 30–31 cites research showing that daughters of single parents are 53 percent more likely to marry as teenagers, 111 percent more likely to have children as teenagers, 164 percent more likely to have a premarital birth, and 92 percent more likely to dissolve their own marriages. Their Chapter 2, "Problems of Mother-Only Families," offers a succint summary of the problems. See also David Blankenhorn, *op. cit.* Chapter 2, "Fatherless Society."

16. McLanahan and Booth, *op. cit.*

17. A comprehensive study performed on 1988 data found that children raised in disrupted or never-married families are at increased risk of academic and behavioral problems, in comparison with children in intact families with both biological parents present. Deborah A. Dawson, "Family Structure and Children's Health and Well-Being: Data from the 1988 National Health Interview

Survey on Child Health," *Journal of Marriage and the Family* 53 (August 1991): 573–84. Similar results were found by Judith S. Wallerstein, Shauna B. Corbin, and Julia M. Lewis, "Children of Divorce: A 10-Year Study," in E. Mavis Hetherington and Josephine D. Arasteh, *Impact of Divorce, Single Parenting and Stepparenting on Children* (Hillsdale: NJ: Lawrence Erlbaum Associates, 1988): 197–214. This is a follow-up study of fifty-two couples and their children who had been divorced ten years previously. Among those who had been latent and adolescent at the time of divorce (now 19–29), only two-thirds were in college or had graduated from college or were seeking advanced degrees. (The national norm is that 85 percent of high school grads go directly to college.) The authors note that this may be due to an abrupt end to child-support payments at age 18.

18. Suet-Ling Pong, "Family Structure, School Context, and Eighth Grade Math and Reading Achievement," *Journal of Marriage and the Family* 59 (August 1997): 734–46.

19. Dawson, *op. cit.*

20. Nicholas Zill, "Behavior, Achievement and Health Problems Among Children in Stepfamilies: Findings from a National Survey of Child Health," in Hetherington and Arasteh, *op. cit.*, 325–68.

21. Dawson, *op. cit.*

22. Frank L. Mott, Lori Kowalski-Jones, and Elizabeth Menaghen, "Paternal Absence and Child Behavior: Does a Child's Gender Make a Difference?" *Journal of Marriage and the Family* 59 (February 1997): 103–18.

23. One might wonder whether the causation runs in the other direction. That is, instead of a child having problems because his father is uninvolved, perhaps the father has withdrawn from a child who already has problems. It is easy to imagine this scenario in a stepfamily, in which a resentful child refuses to accept the new parent, and the adult withdraws in frustration. However, the interpretation that father involvement, per se, is important is supported by the wide-ranging evidence on completely or mostly absent fathers.

24. Paul R. Amato and Fernando Rivera, "Paternal Involvement and Children's Behavior Problems," *Journal of Marriage and the Family* 61 (May 1999): 375–84.

25. Elizabeth C. Cooksey and Michelle M. Fondell, "Spending Time With His Kids: Effects of Family Structure on Fathers' and Children's Lives," *Journal of Marriage and the Family* 58 (August 1996): 693–707. For pre-teens, there was a statistically significant negative impact on grades of living in a single-father household,

or living with a step-father who has biological children living in the same household. For teens, the statistically significant negative impact came from living either in a single-father household, or in a household with a step-father who does not have biological children in the household.

26. Bogenschneider, Karen, "Parental Involvement in Adolescent Schooling: A Proximal Process with Transcontextual Validity," *Journal of Marriage and the Family* 59 (August 1997): 718–33.

27. Ibid., 725, 728.

28. Ibid., 731. The full citations for the works cited by Bogenschneider are C. Simich-Dudgeon, "Increasing Student Achievement through Teacher Knowledge about Parent Involvement," in N.F. Chavkin, ed. *Families and Schools in a Pluralistic Society* (New York: State University of New York Press, 1993): 189–203 and M.B. Smith, "School and Home: Focus on Achievement," in A.H. Passow, ed., *Developing Programs for the Educationally Disadvantaged* (New York: Teachers College Press): 87–107.

29. Pong, *op. cit.*

30. James S. Coleman, "Social Capital in the Creation of Human Capital," *American Journal of Sociology* 94 (1988): 95–S120.

31. This is conceptual framework used in N.M. Astone and S.S. McLanahan, "Family Structure, Parental Practices, and High School Completion," *American Sociological Review* (1991): 309–20. Obviously, this characterization is consistent with the major argument of the present paper.

32. James S. Coleman and T. B. Hoffer, *Public and Private High Schools: The Impact of Communities* (New York: Basic Books, 1987).

33. Pong, *op. cit.*

34. Doris R. Entwisle and Karl L. Alexander, "Family Type and Children's Growth in Reading and Math over the Primary Grades," *Journal of Marriage and the Family* 58 (May 1996): 341–55.

35. Patricia Morgan, *Who Needs Parents? The Effects of Childcare and Early Education on Children in Britain and the USA* (London: The Institute for Economic Affairs, 1996): 69, 79, and especially the Appendix, "Working Through Parents," 128–29.

36. Frank. L. Mott, "Developmental Effects of Infant Care: The Mediating Role of Gender and Health," *Journal of Social Issues* 47, no. 2 (1991): 139–58. Also see Judith L. Rubenstein and Carollee Howes, "Social-Emotional Development of Toddlers in Day Care: The Role of Peers and of Individual Differences," in Sally Kilmer, ed., *Advances in Early Education and Day Care* (Greenwich, Conn: JAI Press, 1983): 13–46.

37. Peter Barglow, Brian E. Vaughn, and Nancy Molitor, "Effects of

Maternal Absence Due to Employment on the Quality of Infant-Mother Attachment in a Low-Risk Sample," *Child Development* 58 (1987): 945–54. Jay Belsky and Michael J. Rovine, "Non-Maternal Care in the First Year of Life and the Security of Infant-Parent Attachment," *Child Development* 59 (1988): 157–67. Belsky and David Eggebeen, "Early and Extensive Maternal Employment and Young Children's Socioemotional Development: Children of the National Longitudinal Survey of Youth," *Journal of Marriage and the Family* 53 (November 1991): 1083–110.

38. The NICHD Early Child Care Research Network, "The Effects of Infant Child Care on Infant-Mother Attachment Security: Results of the NICHD Study of Early Child Care," *Child Development* 68, no. 5 (October 1997): 860–79. Quote from p. 876.

39. Jay Belsky, Sharon Woodworth, and Keith Crnic, "Trouble in the Second Year: Three Questions about Family Interaction," *Child Development* 67 (1996): 556–78. Also see the NICHD Early Child Care Research Network, "Early Child Care and Self-Control, Compliance, and Problem Behavior at Twenty-Four and Thirty-Six Months," *Child Development* 69, no. 4 (August 1998): 1145–70.

40. Patrick F. Fagan and Robert Rector, "The Effects of Divorce on America," *The Heritage Foundation Backgrounder*, no. 1373, Washington, D.C., June 5, 2000.

Contributors

ROBERT J. BARRO is a senior fellow at the Hoover Institution and the Robert C. Waggoner professor of economics at Harvard University. His expertise is in the areas of macroeconomics, economic growth, and monetary theory. Current research interests include the determinants of economic growth, with special emphasis on the role of political institutions. His books include *Determinants of Economic Growth: A Cross-Country Empirical Study, Getting It Right: Markets and Choices in a Free Society*, and *Economic Growth* (coauthor). He is on the executive committee of the American Economic Association, is a fellow of the American Academy of Arts and Sciences and the Econometric Society, an associate of the National Bureau of Economic Research, and a member of the Mont Pelerin Society. Barro received a Ph.D. in economics from Harvard University and a B.S. in physics from Caltech.

GARY S. BECKER is the Rose-Marie and Jack R. Anderson senior fellow at the Hoover Institution and professor of economics and sociology at the University of Chicago. A recipient of the Nobel Memorial Prize in economic sciences in 1992, he was named a recipient of the National Medal of

Science in November of 2000 for his work in social policy. His current research focuses on habits and addictions, formation of preferences, human capital, and population growth. His most recent publications include *The Economics of Life* (with Guity Nashat) and *Accounting for Tastes*. He is a featured monthly columnist for *Business Week*. He holds honorary degrees from a dozen universities, including Hebrew University in Jerusalem, Knox College, Princeton University, Columbia University, and the University of Chicago. Becker received an A.B. (summa cum laude) from Princeton University, and a Ph.D. and A.M. from the University of Chicago.

ANDREW J. COULSON is a senior research associate of the Social Philosophy and Policy Center and author of the book *Market Education: The Unknown History*. He has written numerous articles and essays for academic journals and for newspapers such as the *Wall Street Journal* and the *Seattle Times*. His research aims, by comparing how well various systems have worked across time and around the world, to identify the sort of school system best able to fulfill the public's goals and ideals.

ROBERT E. HALL is the Robert and Carole McNeil joint professor in the Department of Economics at Stanford University and a senior fellow at the Hoover Institution. His research interests include levels of activity in market economics and the economics of high technology. He is coauthor of *Macroeconomics: Theory, Performance and Policy* with John Taylor and *Economics: Principles and Applications* with Marc Lieberman. Hall serves the National Bureau of Economic Research as director of the research program on economic fluctuations and growth and chair of the bureau's Committee on Business Cycle Dating. He is a fellow of the American Academy of Arts and Sciences and the Econometric Society. Hall received his B.A. from the University of California at Berkeley and his Ph.D. from the Massachusetts Institute of Technology.

EDWARD P. LAZEAR is the Jack Steele Parker professor of human resources at Stanford University's Graduate School of Business and a senior fellow at the Hoover Institution. He is the founding and present editor of the *Journal of Labor Economics* and a fellow of the American Academy of Arts and Sciences, the Econometric Society, and the National Bureau of Economic Research. He is former president of the Society of Labor Economics. His book *Personnel Economics* reflects his extensive work on labor markets and personnel issues. He has published eight books and over one hundred papers. He has advised the governments of Czechoslovakia, Romania, Russia, and Ukraine, and received the Leo Melamed Biennial Prize for outstanding research. He received A.B. and A.M. degrees from the University of California at Los Angeles and his Ph.D. in economics from Harvard University.

JENNIFER ROBACK MORSE is a research fellow at the Hoover Institution. Her research interests focus on the family and the free society. She is a columnist for *Forbes Magazine* and the *National Catholic Register* and was a founding member of the academic advisory boards of the Acton Institute for the Study of Religion. Her recently published book, *Love and Economics: Why the Laissez-Faire Family Doesn't Work,* discusses the issue of the family as a necessary building block for a free society. Morse received her Ph.D. in economics from the University of Rochester and spent a postdoctoral year at the University of Chicago.

PAUL M. ROMER is the STANCO 25 professor of economics in the Graduate School of Business at Stanford University and a senior fellow of the Hoover Institution. He was the lead developer of "new growth theory," which provides a foundation for business- and government-thinking about the dynamics of wealth creation. In 1997, Romer was named one of America's twenty-five most influential people by *Time Magazine*. He is a fellow of the American Academy of Arts and Sciences and the Econometric Society and a research associate with the National Bureau of Economic Research. Romer holds a Ph.D. in economics from the University of Chicago.

GEORGE P. SHULTZ, sixtieth secretary of state of the United States, is the first Thomas W. and Susan B. Ford distinguished fellow at the Hoover Institution and Jack Steele Parker professor of international economics at the Graduate School of Business at Stanford University. He has received the Medal of Freedom, the Seoul Peace Prize, and the Koret Prize for Contributions to Economic Reform and Development in Israel. He headed the Reagan Economic Policy Advisory Board and serves on a number of corporate boards. Among his publications are *Economic Policy Beyond the Headlines*; *Turmoil and Triumph: My Years as Secretary of State*; and a recent monograph, *Economics in Action: Ideas, Institutions, Policies*. Shultz holds honorary degrees from the universities of Notre Dame, Loyola, Pennsylvania, Rochester, Princeton, Carnegie-Mellon, City University of New York, Yeshiva, Northwestern, Tel Aviv, Weizmann Institute, Baruch College, Hebrew University of Jerusalem, Tbilisi State, and Keio University in Tokyo. He received a B.A. from Princeton and a Ph.D. in industrial economics from the Massachusetts Institute of Technology.

THOMAS SOWELL is the Rose and Milton Friedman senior fellow in public policy at the Hoover Institution. He writes on economics, history, social policy, ethnicity, and the history of ideas. His most recent books are *A Personal Odyssey*, *Barbarians Inside the Gates,* and *The Quest for Cosmic Justice*, and his writings have appeared in scholarly journals in economics, law, and other fields. His current research focuses on cultural history in a world perspective. His nationally syndicated column appears in more than 170 newspapers from Boston to Honolulu. He received a B.A. in economics (magna cum laude) at Harvard, an M.A. from Columbia University, and a Ph.D. in economics from the University of Chicago in 1968.

SHELBY STEELE is a research fellow at the Hoover Institution who specializes in the study of race relations, multiculturalism, and affirmative action. He received the National Book Critics' Circle Award in the general nonfiction category for his book *The Content of Our Character: A New Vision of Race in America*. He writes for the *New York Times*, the *Wall Street Journal*, and *Harper's Magazine*. His documentary *Seven Days in Bensonhurst* received an Emmy Award, the Writer's Guild Award, and the San Francisco Film Festival Award for television documentary writing. Steele holds a B.A. in political science from Coe College, an M.A. in sociology from Southern Illinois University, and a Ph.D. in English from the University of Utah.

Index